WAYMAKING

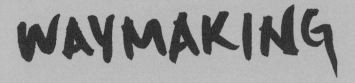

WAYMAKING

AN ANTHOLOGY OF WOMEN'S ADVENTURE WRITING, POETRY AND ART

EDITED BY
Helen Mort
Claire Carter
Heather Dawe
Camilla Barnard

Vertebrate Publishing, Sheffield
www.v-publishing.co.uk

WAYMAKING

Edited by Helen Mort, Claire Carter, Heather Dawe and Camilla Barnard

First published in 2018 by Vertebrate Publishing. Reprinted in 2020 and 2022.
VERTEBRATE PUBLISHING
Omega Court, 352 Cemetery Road, Sheffield S11 8FT, United Kingdom.
www.v-publishing.co.uk

Front cover illustration – Jane Beagley.
Part-title illustrations – Tessa Lyons.

A CIP catalogue record for this book is available from the British Library.

ISBN: 978-1-910240-75-5 (Paperback)
ISBN: 978-1-910240-76-2 (Ebook)

10 9 8 7 6 5 4 3

Design and production by Jane Beagley.

www.v-publishing.co.uk

Vertebrate Publishing is committed to printing on paper from sustainable
sources.

Printed and bound in Europe by Latitude Press.

Contents

UNION

A Note from the Editors

'Hero stories are wearing thin. We have lived a male life, we have lived within the patriarchy. It's something else to take ownership of your own story.' – JANE CAMPION
THE GUARDIAN, 20 MAY 2018

The idea for *Waymaking* came about during a run. For a short while Helen and I both worked in central Leeds, we met up once a week to run at lunchtime, heading from the university, through Headingley's ginnels, along hidden trails to the woods on the north-western edge of the city.

We would talk about many things as we ran, but one of the things we most keenly discussed was what a woman's narrative of wild adventure would look like. And by 'narrative' we were thinking prose, poetry, visual art; there are so many ways to express the creativity inspired by being outdoors.

While there are accomplished female writers and artists out there – and we have early pioneers like Nan Shepherd and Gwen Moffat to look to – I think our voices are often not heard above the, at times, clichéd stories of men conquering mountains, rock faces and other wild places.

We wanted to explore this more, and got talking with Claire, a poet and filmmaker then working at Vertebrate Publishing, who was very supportive. *Waymaking* was born. After speaking with Jon Barton at Vertebrate to see whether he would be interested in publishing such a book, a website was built and the call-out for contributions began in earnest. The submissions were surprising and recognisable, active and still, participatory and observational. Women were voicing and marking all sorts of narratives from the outdoor and the wild.

Roll forward a few years and here we are, with a successful

Kickstarter campaign and generous support from Alpkit. This book wouldn't have happened without Vertebrate taking it on, bringing our ideas and everyone's contributions to print. Camilla has been a great editor for the book; her enthusiastic, considered and honest thoughts certainly helped to shape my contribution for the better.

At the heart of *Waymaking* is a desire to encourage more women to express their love of the wild and adventure, and to get these voices heard. All royalties will be split equally between two charities: Rape Crisis and the John Muir Trust. Thank you to everyone who contributed and to everyone who has supported this book. We hope you like what you read and see.

Running with no steps or breaths.
Climbing with no moves.
Watching without thinking.
Sharing without judging.
Dancing without caring.
A day spent without a narrative.
No failure, no success.
Pure absorption. – HAZEL FINDLAY, *NO-SELF*

I grew up in love with everything outdoors, and most
particularly with Dartmoor, where my grandparents lived
and where we'd spend our holidays tramping from tor to tor,
swimming in the ice-cold Dart and scrambling up and down
scree. That wild, upland landscape is still the wellspring of
my imagination. Everything I write is rooted in landscape
and nature; yet it remains a genre dominated by men. Part
of the problem is the barriers women often face in becoming
a protagonist in a world removed from the domestic or
the professional. Yet given half a chance – and perhaps a
courageous example to follow, like the women in this book –
we can move through the world just as freely as men.

Some years ago I gave a talk about the process of writing
my second novel, a process during which I set out alone
to walk north up the A5 for four days and three nights. To
be clear, I didn't wild-camp: I booked B&Bs and pubs and
simply walked between them, and in busy suburban England
there wasn't even any possibility that I could have got lost.
Yet while it pales into insignificance measured against the
adventures described in this collection, this simple trip still
felt like a challenge because it meant, at every stage, going
against what other people believed I should do.

After the talk, a woman approached me: 'I could *never* do that,' she said, shaking her head. 'Of course you could, if you really wanted to,' I replied with an encouraging smile. 'Oh no, I honestly couldn't – I'd be way too scared. And my husband wouldn't like it, anyway.'

The stories women are told – and which we also tell ourselves – about what is safe or acceptable or possible for us reflect neither our true capabilities or the risks the world really presents. They are stories that contain and circumscribe us and make us fearful; they deny us our full agency, our right to gamble; they keep our world small, and often domestic. The irony, of course, is that it is in the domestic that so frequently the greatest danger waits.

What does it look like when despite these narratives women go out and take up our full space in the world; when we answer a need to come into relationship with wild places in a way that is unmediated by guardians or gatekeepers; or when we push our bodies and minds to places that are impossible to find indoors? These words and images are a glimpse of that world seen through the eyes of women who may not think of themselves as pioneers – may in fact shrug that label off, or point to others, anyone but themselves – but who, for those of us yet unsure, or hesitant, are exactly that.

And there's something else this collection demonstrates. The 'female relationship' with nature and landscape is often described as more spiritual, more physical and embodied, or more nurturing than the male encounter. But those seeking an essentialist view of how women relate to wild places – one in which women as a group share certain experiences and preferences relating to the natural world, experiences and preferences which perhaps can be discovered by reading this book – may be disappointed. The voices and perspectives in *Waymaking* are radical precisely for their sheer variety, something that demonstrates the profound and manifest truth that the female experience of the wild – like all female experiences – is simply the human one; which is, like humans, infinitely varied.

In *Waymaking* you will find women seeking solitude and women travelling in company; women out to conquer and women who need to commune; women who are fearless, and women battling their fear; women who are mothers, daughters, wives and lovers, and women who tell us nothing about those parts of their lives; white women, women of colour and First Nation women; women of deep faith and of none; bruised, broken and heartsore women, and women focused only on how their skill and their sinews and muscles can carry them up, over, into and away.

Climbing, running, wild swimming, skiing, mountain biking, sailing, working and walking everywhere from Cumbria to Antarctica, the Alps to Alaska, Patagonia to Wyoming and Ireland to Australia, meet the adventurers, the waymakers, the women who have found their place in the wild world: '*All of them, out there, in the sun/and wind, making their way/under the tremendous*', as Ruth Wiggins writes.

May they inspire you to do the same.

MELISSA HARRISON
Suffolk, April 2018

VICINITY

Gravel road, once short
stretches hot, sore and dusty.
A stranger points: *fountain*.

Paella for one?
She says: *walk with heart open –*
brave like Dorothy.

On the edge of town:
a roadside flasher – no one around,
I push on.

Can I walk with you?
He laughs: too many miles to make
to wait for me.

From their messy stick nests
on each stone church in each village
storks ring their flat bells.

Snapshots from the Camino de Santiago
CATH DRAKE

Lost in the Light

TARA KRAMER

I'm starting to measure time as it's marked by the ice caps. Two months here, three months there, then fall in Montana, or spring, or a month of summer, and then again to the Flat White. I scatter through the seasons and across hemispheres, losing myself in the months, the landscape, the cold and the heat.

I've worked for seven seasons at the poles running research camps in Greenland and Antarctica. I'm growing accustomed to bending from here to there and there to here, but I still stagger. My body in the heat, my mind with the months. I say winter when I mean summer. April when it's October. In June I boarded a cargo plane on the Greenland ice cap in the balmy 17 °F summer, and thirty-six hours later I stood sweating on the kerb, at midnight, hailing a taxi from Madison Square Garden. The disorientation I find on the ice travels with me.

Some days, when the light is flat and the snow without shadows, I live as if inside a ping-pong ball. The clouds overtake the sky. The horizon fades. The sparkle, the wind waves patterned in the snow, the delicate blues and muted greys dissolve into a smoky haze. The landless landscape turns to eggshell white, and the drifts I otherwise avoid become memories. I walk from my tent to breakfast, feeling with my feet. Blinking, blinking, blinking. I stare at remnants of shadows and shuffle one foot in front of the other, sometimes tripping to my knees as I bump an invisible cornice. I am lost in the light as one feels lost in the dark.

In West Antarctica I groom the three miles of skiway in a Tucker Sno-Cat before complete flat light falls upon us. In my weather observation I report the surface definition as 'poor'. Not yet 'nil', but nearly. I can still follow the line from my previous pass, but only if I strain at the several feet of snow just in front of the tracks. Squinting, leaning forward in my seat, forehead pressed against the glass. For three, four, five hours, there's only single-minded concentration. Only the pacing of back and forth and back and forth, without having left one place or arrived at another. I exit the skiway, my mind numb and empty.

Eventually the grey breaks. The clouds part and reveal a clear blue stretching as a dome above camp. I follow the infinite line of the horizon encircling me. Now, in this light, I see emptiness expanding like an open-ended question. The ice sheet is a mass of continuity biting at my cheeks. My body pressed closely against its haunting calm, I stare into the void encountered at the edge of a cliff. At first I am overtaken by a sinking sensation and then by the horrifying, irrational urge to jump. I back away and hide in the dark of a sleeping bag, in books, in strong coffee and conversation. I find something to hold tight to. I try to sit down and reground myself. But inevitably I creep back to the edge and continue peering into the alluring abyss. Those hundreds and hundreds of miles of ice stretching boldly to the coast. In this seemingly eternal light and boundless space, the Flat White reflects the palette of my mind. Exposed, raw, unshielded.

I have no concept of this space. I cannot fathom this emptiness. At times I've fantasised about indefinitely walking away from camp and out into that wide open. I'd tuck my chin and turn my head against the wind, the cold stinging the sliver of skin exposed between my hat and gaiter. I'd hold up my hood and lumber through that crust like sand. Maybe then I would understand that depth of space. I told a friend of this delusion after having spent two months in the Flat White with only four people. He had just arrived at camp and responded, 'Tara, you've been here too long'. Yes, that's possible. But ice sheets have their way of releasing me.

From time, and expectations, and even my own sense of
place. After months living on snow, two miles above land,
I feel liberated, drifting on this frozen sea.

Despite my incapacity to comprehend the sheer expanse,
this landscape is not truly empty. It's snow. And ice. And
wind. There are ice crystals floating and blowing here. This
is a glacier. A place defined by the starkness of its uniformity.
A place that reveals the most critical climate records in the
world. *This* is why scientists and we as staff toil to come and
then labour to exist here. Heating food, melting snow for
drinking water, sleeping in tents at -50° Fahrenheit. Daily
living asks nearly everything of us. These ice sheets, they
want to get rid of us, bury us in drifts, scour away our very
existence. Everything we bring here gets ravaged, blasted and
inundated and cracked by vicious, relentless wind. *Go. Away.*
This place seems to say to me, *You do not belong here.*

My family and friends and even co-workers say there's
nothing here. *Why would you want to go there?* I, too, often
wonder why. But I know that on the ice, all else fades away.
There are no trails to run, no trees or stores, no text messages
to answer. There are few distractions, and those that exist –
the movie nights, dominoes, knitting – they only occupy
my mind for so long. The ice sheet is an abyss from which
I cannot walk.

I learn to be where I am. To keep going. In the thirty-
knot winds, four coats, three pairs of pants, neck gaiter, nose
gaiter, goggles, two hats, and three-pound boots. Stumbling
through drifts, with ice in my hair, on my way to lunch, in
August. Once I mumbled out loud against the wall of wind,
'Sometimes there's wind, sometimes there's rain. Sometimes
you do not arrive when you're ready to have gotten there.'

Here, I breathe.

Iceberg
DEZIREE WILSON

The beauty and harmony of water and ice formations belie their hazardous nature. Dangerous and ruthless beauty makes an alluring narrative.

Abstract compositions like this seem to find their own rhythm, independent of any active thinking on my part. I lose myself in the ebb and flow of the form and emerge from a daydream with an image in front of me that I have no conscious recollection of having created.

Steinbock

ANJA KONIG

The upper lake is dammed. I know
Tödi, the mountain in the distance.

The lower lake is drained,
a shadowy stain in the rock basin.

Rusting pipes wait, numbered,
wide like giant iron mushrooms.

The cable car can carry forty tons.
I see it clawing a lorry,

turbine blades
like dinosaur wings.

On the way down ibex
lower their ridged horns

foraging in scree. A whistle
or scream warns them of me.

[untitled 1]
KRYSTLE WRIGHT

As an adventure photographer, capturing moments from the field, I have always believed in finding the balance between the athlete and their environment. After all, the adventure cannot take place without the environment surrounding. During a two-week expedition on the Barnard Glacier in the Wrangell St Elias Mountains in Alaska, Sheldon Kerr leads the way ahead of Erin Smart and Lindsay Mann to discover potential new lines to ski. It's important when capturing athletes in these grand landscapes that they don't become a standing statue; instead, it's about finding those key moments to showcase how the athletes interact with the landscape, in this case, through ski mountaineering.

Enchantment Larches

NIKKI FRUMKIN

It was so cold my paint froze as I applied it to the paper. At the end of the night I had a thick layer of ice across the whole painting. I ran my fingers across it and it felt like a frozen pond. In the morning I saw the ice had melted and dried, leaving ice patterns in the paint of the sky.

I carried this paper around for four days, twenty-two miles and 2,100 metres. I painted through sunset and into the next day. The sky turned pink and dark purple; it was beautiful. All the larches were golden yellow. We don't get colours this magical in the city and they were hard to leave.

On the hike out I took a fall between two icy boulders, and this painting wedged me in between them, keeping me from slipping all the way down the slabby ramp. I was able to crawl out of my backpack on to sure footing, and remove the pack and painting from the rocks where it was stuck. It left only a tiny wrinkle in the top left of the painting, but it probably saved me some serious scrapes. I never thought my art would double as climbing protection, but I sure do like that idea. This one is special.

Mountains of the Mourne
PENELOPE SHUTTLE

Slieve Donard   *mountain land*

Slieve Binnian   *stone glints off wet rock*

Slieve Commedagh   *forgotten quarry roads*

Slievenaglogh   *ghosts of golden eagles*

Ben Crom and Slieve Muck   *a granite wall*

Slieve Lamagan   *twenty-two miles long*

Wee Binnian   *tracking round*

The Mournes   *keeping nothing*

Hare's Gap   *and no one*

Percy Bysshe and the Hole of the Sprites   *out*

Fairfield from Wansfell

PAULA DUNN

I try to avoid painting familiar views and prefer to focus on compositions from an elevated perspective where people generally have to walk to be able to enjoy. The light and weather are also key, as they will turn a very flat landscape into something more dynamic and dramatic.

This painting is inspired by a lovely autumnal walk from Ambleside to Wansfell via Troutbeck. At the end of the walk you reach the top of Wansfell, where, on a good day, you are rewarded by a fantastic view of Ambleside and the surrounding area. On this day we could see for miles and there were so many things perfectly aligned: weather, light and the autumnal colours of the landscape. There was so much about this view that inspired me, as I was at the time focusing on a series of work which related to isolation – a fascination with how people carve out an existence in the most isolated places where the weather has such an impact on the landscape.

Eglwyseg Day

JEAN ATKIN

[11.09 a.m.]
path up through wind-clipped gorse, wind in the eye
& such yellow splashes through the heather

sheep-cropped mounds & sink-holes of the mines
all smooth as china cups & saucers stacked up

at the table edge
& shelved up there, the purple hills;
here, bilberries & our purple fingers.

[12.23 p.m.]
share coffee from the Thermos. Perch
on springy bones of heather root & watch

across the gorge, a nursery
of dark firs gathered quiet
by the cliff's white knee

we listen to the nudge
of a sheep through whinberries

& hum of a bee-line into warm air.

[1.53 p.m.]
path divides into two green trails. We know
we have chosen the right way when

we can look down on the other as it narrows to a thread,
full-stopped at a brink by a sleeping sheep.

Berries are red-dangled, plumping above pale screes.
We halt by a jut of stones

where a twist of swallows dives & feasts
on insect-clouds blown

      from Eglwyseg's lips.

[2.45 p.m.]
beyond: raised tide of Llantysilio's hills
& near, like a little adder striped & scaled,

a brown caterpillar inches in the dust. Thistles
are spent, dying in their upright stalks

& at our backs the moor rolls up to Ruabon,
above an oblique shine

      of thistledown, loose cloak of looms & riddles.

[3.03 p.m.]
fresh gulley water bubbles in a sink
of stone, then falls & empties back

inside the hollow hill. It leaves no sound.
We walk past a vole passage drilled through dung.

A fence-line stitches the grouse moor. Eyes stop
on a fencepost with tilted crow.

Bronze Age burial kist, mapped once, gone now.

[3.56 p.m.]
spreadeagled by the wall, a dead sheep, chalky
porous vertebrae in rainwashed fleece

we pass three daisies low along the path, like dropped
white pebbles from children's pockets

& the mountain rears & grins,
shows all its caried limestone teeth.

Affric

ALISON GRANT

It was mostly distance,
not the kind you could measure,
but simply crossing the bealach at Kintail,
carrying everything
to camp out well above the river
amongst the shielings looped around with green-dunged grass,
waking in the slipstream of a night
that never really darkened,
the damp sedge twitching with wide-eyed frogs.

And then this morning,
leaving the car and walking into fog,
heelprints denting the snow,
the sun pressing against the mist
until the sky is sudden blue,
Sgùrr na Lapaich punching through
the low cloud and haloed pine,
the frost bristling across the grey stone,
each rock a world of its own, relic and habitat.

Walking Moses Trod

PAM WILLIAMSON

Moses Trod [trod: an indistinct path, a desire line] is part of my Pass Book series of paintings. I made expeditions to investigate and respond to the ancient ways through the mountains – the passes, not the peaks.

Moses was reputed to be a Honister quarryman, working in the days before metalled roads opened up new routes through the Lake District fells. He hauled his split slate using ponies and sleds, in the least stressful way through the mountains to Wasdale, then descended to the sea and the waiting boats. Stories tell how in addition to exporting slate, Moses smuggled out his home-distilled whisky which he concealed on the slopes of Great Gable.

My response to this atmospheric tale and walk are four paintings connected by the shape of the route making its way in verse across the canvases.

i Mine to Mountain

Honister passage of rock
boots on stone
rattle underfoot
horizons expand
slate clouds slate land
quarry scar
Fleetwith
burrowed split transported
Moses trod this way
boots on stone
rattle underfoot
mine to mountain

ii Sledgate

Moses trod this way
boots on stone
rattle underfoot
horizons lengthen
slate way sledgate
dense resisting
dragged through contours
geology in motion
to water and to sea
boots on stone
rattle underfoot
man moves mountains

iii Trod

Moses trod
winding through mountains
clutching skirts of Brandreth
hoisted over bogs
ducking under shattered crags
Gables Green and Great
linked yet parted
windblown gap
clouds blow
secrets hidden
only boots on stone
rattle underfoot

iv Scree to Sea

Moses trod this way
boots on stone
rattle underfoot
wet swirl of cloud
Beck Head watershed.
Moses Finger beckons
water gleams
gravity propels the way
water glitters
skyline jagged
ancient landscape over
man moving mountains

Murmuration

DR JUDY KENDALL

murmurat e mathical ch
gathering its neighbours as po
changes in speed or direction. As a p
magnified and distorted by those surrounding
patterns. Why? Survival. To avoid flying predators, they seek
in flocks and trying to avoid the edge of the group. Still glorsscop
"ion" of starlings is pure mathematical chaos (larger shapes compo
infinitely varied smaller patterns). Each bird flies as close to its neighb ours as
copying changes in speed or direction. As a result, tiny deviations by one bird ar
magnified and distorted by those surr ounding it, creating rippling, swirling pa
y? Survival. To avoid flying predators,temat seek safetyinnumbers,gathering in f
flocks and trying to avoid the edge ofibleth Still glorious. A murmuration" of la
starlings is pure mathematical chaos i cr(lar composed of infinitely varied sm
patterns). Each bird flies as close to I resre ts nbours as possible, copying chan
speed or direction. As a result, tiny dev saf i one bird are magnified and larger
distorted by those surrounding it, creat ious. A rippling, swirling patterns. infi?it
To avoid flying predators, they seek saf sed of sib numbers, gathering in flocks o
trying to avoid the edge of the group. e p tteThan composed of infinitel distorted
is pure mathematical chaos (larger s os Each bird flies as close to i sscop hem ey
patterns). Each bird flies as close to tiny deviations by one biafTo avoi istor se
in speed or direction. As a result, ti lo eating, rippling,   swirlir fl ying ure
and distorted by those surroundin tryafety in numb   ers, alro up s p
Why? Survival. To avoid flying pre ed ing to av   oid the sh
gathering in flocks and trying to ge of the grou   p whne ighb
glorious. A "murmuration" of sta   mat Still glor   ious. P ure
   (larger shapes composed of infi as close t   o it as   poss
      bird flies as close to its copying cha   nages r esult
      speed or direction. As   speed o   r dir a, ted
   magnified and distorted by t th   ose   rou
   and d swirling patterns. Why? Su   rv s gie
   the seek safety in numbers, isto   ) neixrns
   direct starlings edge of the g   gathagnif
   of infinitely is pure mat   ednydeviati m
   to its neighboursvaried sma   nges hb ts
      ion. As a result, magnif as po   ur, r
         rippling, swirilng pa   i
         predators, th
         flocks and tryi
            ng t glorio
            us. A mur
         mathemat nf com
            ical c i initely vari pure m
               e flies as tglorious.ing to
                  copying chan result, tipnat
                  ny d magnified a it,cre
                  x rvival. T safeating Su
                  ty in try

Signs

GERALDINE GREEN

The feathers were still there.

Pattern of grey-black, pointing this way and that on the side of the common. I counted twenty of them below gorse bushes whose flowers have yet to blaze Birkrigg with their golden glow, their scent of coconut.

No sign of a struggle, bloody body, broken wings.

In the hard, clear light of evening the Scafell range pokes summits through low, white clouds stark against the northern horizon. Coniston Old Man, Dow Crag, Wetherlam loom sharp and heavy as slate on Hoad's shoulder.

I have one of the feathers in my pocket.

Brimmerhead Farmhouse

PAULA DUNN

This painting probably should be named 'The day we didn't quite get up to Fairfield'! It is from a failed attempt to walk the Fairfield Horseshoe on a beautiful crisp March morning after snowfall the night before. It was a glorious day with beautiful clear skies, fresh snow and only a handful of people who had the same idea as us. Unfortunately, the clear skies did not last very long and we soon had to turn back after Great Rigg when snow – more like a blizzard – started to fall again, but before we did I managed to capture lots of images of the wonderful views looking across to Grasmere.

Last Night I Dream we Walk up to the Point Again

IMOGEN CASSELS

climbing to the summit of the hill
on a spotless afternoon, the earth glowing
like lit malachite, while eye-like flowers,
blue, yellow, pink, watch quietly

lost in heather it's so easy to become still

a trio of burns run down to the shore,
translucent sisters, brown with stones.
we lift teasel-buds to our lips
and smoke them

small, slate birds leelooing on the cliff edge

the sea rolls in and water fills
our eyes, ears, mouths, bones,
turning us to statues, standing, looking out,
cobalt in the saline air

if we leave, the island comes with us

To Reach Green Before Dark

LILACE MELLIN GUIGNARD

She hadn't realised how quiet America could be, even with the
radio's squall and windows scrolled to nothing. After four years
of higher ed., watching the wilderness on TV, reading about it in
white men's journals, it was reassuring to discover stretches of
such contented silence. Like Lewis and Clark, she would make
her mark, slash south-east to north-west across the territory.
The common, unfamiliar ground visible outside the truck cab
and in the small slabs of mirror soothed, like a good book
found at a party where your ride's in the back room with the
host's best buddy, her purse full of condoms and the car keys.

On those grey ribbons which bind this oddly divided
package of democracy, politics takes a backseat to geography,
capitalism scoots over for capitals. Only the land's loose
embrace can reach her here. No stopping, she promises
herself (and her mother), for men hitching free rides. This
trip is all hers, a cruising down the future's memory lane.
She'll take snapshots of mule deer and prairie dogs, bison
and bears. Maps are puzzles, games she can't lose.

Driving for days she observes how the sky changes along
with state lines, ecosystems, accents and roadkill. No more
slow southern vowels. Fewer dead skunks, more deer and
dog carcasses. Used to the gradual bleeding of blue into the
many ridges of home and their cloud-mist meetings, the
Midwest's horizon seems as flat as a mother's scowl when
you thought never to pry her lips apart. In Minnesota, the
tornadoes make the world beyond the window all but vanish.
The only evidence: rain heaved at the windshield. She thinks
it could be possible with practice to identify a place just from
a photo of the sky – like surfers do the coast from where and
how a wave breaks, and farmers know a field.

Texaco attendants provide the little conversation needed. They clean the glass and ask where she's going. She practises not answering, as if there were an answer she could offer were his smile just right and the world a safer place. Never gives her name. This is real … is real … is real … thrumming mantra of her telephone pole road-trance, backdrop to other thoughts just as the buttes lounging on the curved horizon accent the fresh-thrown tumbleweed.

Late May. An RV owner says Montana snowed fourteen inches so she goes north only to Missoula. If it weren't for her small dog and two-wheel drive, she'd have dared the cold. Glacier, a mammoth dream, the park that makes the Sierras seem common, must remain on the border's fence unreckoned. The one place she'd planned to stop and get out. It'd been snug in front when she left the Smoky's fog-smudged dogwoods and endured North Dakota's blitz of billboards promising 300-foot prairie dogs and WALL (just ninety-three miles ahead) DRUG. Always recalling those calendar photos of iced lakes and wild flowers sliding off steep grades, as close to Europe's fjords and Alps as she could drive.

In Idaho, browsing in a lodge gift shop while her cinnamon twist is heated, she strums the fringes of bandanas and jackets with hand-painted state emblems, tanned animals and faces. But who to give them to? She tries to picture her college friends wearing such things and thinking about her here. Not as she is now, not as it really happened. They'd imagine her at the bar with old hunters, learning the local lies, casting bullshit and winks to the bartender bringing a drink from the fella who invites her to hike the gorge at dawn. She takes the warm roll and coffee to go, silently passing the men under animals stuffed and staring. A series of hairpins clung to with sticky fingers and she's in another state.

In the Central Washington desert it hits her: in her freedom she's fabricating reasons. A purpose for doing one thing not another, something to hang emotions on rather than just letting them flutter in air filled with sage and exhaust. She's going eighty trying to reach green before dark, aiming for a peninsula surrounded by cartographers' blue ink. Soon she'll stand on the other coast, actually touch the second bookend, which, like God, she'd always accepted was there without any real proof.

Camped in Olympic National Park, the rainforest is a companionable misfit. Her tent tucked under the mossy boughs of ancient trees – cedar, spruce and hemlock more than a hundred feet high – she dreams she'll die in a field in Montana one night when the stars blind like sun on ice. Rain will have shrunk her blanket to a square barely large enough for one. Somewhere it's dry, and friends crawl in bed with friends.

Up at 3 a.m. she shivers and imagines being held by the man in site 32 who'd borrowed a can opener before dinner and to whom she'd said only what was necessary. Should she have suggested they hike together? Would that raise or lower her risk? The stars poise their frozen tips above her head. Part of her wishes for the world of introductions where she can meet people and not be afraid to linger or walk away. But here in the wilderness, or at least its campground, she loves how there's no one to say, 'I've never seen this side of you before'. Tonight silence simmers. On a log by the unused firepit, she leans towards the uncertain warmth of his tent next door, tracing the long zipper with her eyes. She doesn't mean to tease herself, is already thinking how teeth meet and part predictably, like finding an end to a once endless Montana road that wouldn't have been enough, anyway.

Excerpts from 'La Fuente', an essay
KARI NIELSEN

Evaristo opened the barn door and kneeled beside his sick goat. She quivered and her eyes rolled upwards. Rain reverberated on the tin roof. Evaristo offered me the syringe after he had filled it with medication, tapped the side and pushed the priming liquid out the needle. I reached for it, but he pulled his hand away and smiled. As he injected her hip, she resisted, her hooves scraping the dirt floor. I rubbed her back until Evaristo withdrew the needle.

My climbing partner Joshua and I followed the short, sinewy man along the tight wooden rails of sheep fencing and across the yard. His simple house had been constructed of shakes and expanded with government-issued particle board siding. A skinned mutton leg hung by its ankle beneath the awning. Inside was dark, warm, and smelled distinctly of sheep fat. Evaristo's latest calendar girl held a STIHL pressure washer and wore black stilettos that lengthened her pale legs. The cook-stove occupied most of the kitchen, and the oven door creaked when Evaristo opened it to check on the meat and peeled potatoes. Chelo, his nineteen-year-old son, stood from his stool at the small table to kiss my cheek and shake Joshua's hand.

In his tired shuffle, Evaristo neatly set out metal cups, Nescafé, tea and powdered milk. His acid-washed jeans hung loosely around his thin legs. With worked and leathered hands, he lifted an aluminum tea kettle and filled the *mate* gourd slowly, allowing water to bubble down beneath the yerba. Grinning, he passed me the gourd and then served me a metal cup of home-made strawberry wine. Evaristo shared the mutton and passed a plate of stiff *tortas*, a Patagonian fried bread. Only then would Chelo don his chaps and find his horses so he could pack our gear to the crossing at Río Colonia. Evaristo would be our closest neighbour for the next two months. His *campo*, Tres Limones, was a three-and-a-half-hour walk down the valley from our destination.

Joshua and I had returned to the Chilean Patagonia in order to care-take Jonathan Leidich's homestead, Sol de Mayo, which was cradled at the U-shaped head of Valle Colonia. Jonathan was Joshua's long-time friend from the US and had made the three-hour drive up the valley with us on an improvised road that morning. The previous autumn, he had allowed us to base camp at Sol de Mayo for a ten-day trip so that we could climb Cerro Colonia.

After four months of travelling alone, the oasis of the *campo* had felt like an arrival. My perpetual search for connection to a place had ceased at the isolated refuge of Sol de Mayo. But the essence of the *campo* lingered after I had left Patagonia in May. I had forged an instinctual bond to the place that I could not forget even after seven months in the States. And so Joshua and I returned when I had space and time in my college schedule. Drawn to a life that seemed to be encased in the memory of my birthplace, Montana, I wanted to live the *campo*, to understand the ground's scale, based on my own body's capacities for work and exploration.

Sol de Mayo is situated just over glaciated domes and mountains on the edge of the Northern Patagonian Ice Field in the Aysén region of southern Chile. The land is isolated from both the north and south by two rivers, the Claro and the Colonia, which wall it off from both sides of the valley. Until 2011, when two landowners on the north side of Río Colonia bought trucks and began to drive to their *campos*, access into the valley was limited to horseback.

On the day we arrived at Tres Limones, we finished our lunch and began to walk westwards on the trail, beneath the double-horn summits of Cerro Puño. Forested slopes rapidly rose to a distinct tree line, before glaciers and rocks capped off the peaks. The road ended in less than two hours at the final uninhabited *campo* on the north side of Río Colonia. We waited in a barn until the rain cleared and then navigated the open gravel bar to the river. The caretakers met us with an inflatable kayak at the crossing, and we ferried our packs and the resupply across the river.

Río Claro meets the Colonia just downstream from the crossing. It swoops in an S-curve, its glacial brightness carving into the shore, down to where the clear water meets the churning silt of Río Colonia. A clear line extends downriver from the triangulated apex of the gravel bar that isolates the rivers, dividing blue-green from grey-brown. It zippers up the island of Sol de Mayo with clean finality. We were isolated, cut off by ice and water. We would control who or what moved in or out.

We walked the final forty-five minutes across sand and rock, following the Claro towards the mountains. A loosely closed hand could strip purple and red berries from the abundant *chaura* bushes along the trail. The path finally dipped and turned to reveal a three-sided barn, a corral, a tin-sided house. We walked through a wooden gate, then into a grassy yard where chickens pecked at the ground. The dark and drafty one-room house behind the apple trees would be our home, as it was before. I propped my pack against the inside wall and removed my wet boots.

The caretakers brought us to the three-sided barn and showed us where they kept the animal feed. The dust, greying wood and lingering smell of horse sent my memory to my mother's first partner after her divorce from my father. John was a veterinarian who owned a horse and buffalo ranch on the north side of Bozeman, Montana. The outbuildings and fences had held up to a century of long, snowy winters under his family's name. I remembered walking through a long, dark barn when I was seven,

past a row of tanning buffalo hides still sprinkled with salt.
Dust caked the frosted windows, but the organisation of
saddles, bridles and tools along the walls was immaculate.

My mother loved the idea of this quiet man, of the
romantic past that she saw alive in him. He allowed her to
escape the subdivision where she and my father had created
a life for a short time, before new neighbours added houses
and turned over the tall brown grasses into landscaped lots.
Our new neighbours never came to approve of the chickens
in our yard, nor of my sister's horse that mowed his section
of the three-acre lot down to dirt. John did. He showed us
how to clean fish in alpine streams, pluck the feathers from
the geese we raised, and press apple cider.

Stepping into the Chilean *campo*, I was returning to a life
that I had wilfully forgotten since moving out of my mother's
hard-pressed household at sixteen and then escaping to
Vermont for college. The land-based life-ways that were
being lost to subdivisions, roads and resorts in Montana were
still alive, though threatened, in Aysén. But it wasn't until
I lay the woven blanket, sheepskin cushion and lightweight
saddle on a horse's back at Sol de Mayo that I realised what
brought me back to this place. The smell of dust and hay
propelled me back to the primal sanctuary of my memory.

[…]

I stopped at the gate, where the grass grew tall. A bull's skull
faced the horns of Cerro Puño. Eighteen sheep rested in the
shade of bushes in their pasture. The horses swished their
tails, though the swarming *tábanos* had mellowed in the
cool evening. I had never been so satisfied living within the
bounds of that fence. The Río Claro tumbled while I stood
beneath the protective stare of Puño, a mountain that signifies
where you stand in the world and where you are going.

I slid down the cut bank and stood in the river. The water curled and tripped over rocks on its way out of the valley, into the Colonia, the Baker, the Pacific. The word *claro* is most directly translated as *clear*. Frequently used in conversation, it is a word of encouragement, to express agreement with another's ideas. It is often spoken in the same instances as *verdad*, or *true*. *Claro* is said with a drawn-out 'a', which encourages the other speaker to slow their words. *Claaaaro*. Nothing more needs to be said; the conversation stands as it is. *Claro* is truth.

You could see the Claro's source from Lago Colonia, which is two kilometres north of Sol de Mayo. That open gap to the south remained a blank emptiness in my mind's geography. The wide space that the mountains permitted to the sky, the swift and clean slope of subalpine vegetation that was dotted with rocks, the deep colours reminded me, joyously, of Montana. It was not a painful and nostalgic reminiscence, but a realisation that maybe this place could be home as well: these shrubs, these mountains, this sweeping open sky.

At the end of January, Joshua and I set out on a brief trip to the source of the river, into that empty space.

[...]

The slope mellowed as I met the glacier's spidering crevasses at eye level. A great whip-crack broke the still air. I turned to the glacier, belly dropping, expecting a great sheet of ice to tumble into the lake. Black scree clicked, but nothing more came of it. I continued in silence but remained on edge. Life in the alpine environment had faded, and I had softened.

Evaristo once made an unexpected visit to Sol de Mayo during a resupply. He expectantly sat in the Zodiac as we prepared to cross Lago Colonia. His brown hands held an oar, and he squinted up the shore towards me. In his delicate mumble, he said, '*Quiero conocer el otro lado*' – *I want to know the other side. Conocer,* the verb 'to know', can be used both when seeing a place and also when meeting another person. He wanted to meet the glacier, *la fuente*, the source of the river that outlined his land and existence. Joshua pulled the cord on the outboard. The motor drowned the sound of the waterfalls that fell from Puño's west-facing cliffs. Evaristo put down the oar and crouched, securely rooting to the metal floor.

On the lake's opposite shore, Colonia Glacier had formerly snaked southwards, stripping the land down to bare rock, and then retreated from the lake. Evaristo's crow's-feet crinkled as he looked towards the mountains, where two large glaciers rolled into the barren valley floor.

'What do you think?' I asked.

'It's okay,' he said, drily.

'Do you prefer Tres Limones?'

'*Sí, po.*' Of course. 'Nothing here is green.'

I skipped rocks across the murky surface of Lago Colonia, into the space between the lapping waves, where the shifting and wavering silt snaked around in plumes and feathers and disappeared in the sun. I had smiled at his comment.

At the pass, I saw no long, meandering glacier in the neighbouring watershed, but an endless series of rounded domes rubbed raw by the recent passing of ice. The sun beat down hard against the snagging wind. I did not linger long before retreating back to the vegetated lowlands.

[...]

We followed the horse trail from the river crossing back to Sol de Mayo, exploring the infinite folds of worlds in that single point on the body of the earth. The dirt track eventually followed a collapsing fence line across the open pasture's blonde grass, past the wood lot, and through the grey side gate that creaked upon our entry.

Titcomb Basin

LIZZY DALTON

In the summer of 2017 I embarked on my first solo backpacking trip through Wyoming's Wind River Range. While I am confident in the outdoors, the idea of going on an unsupported trip into one of America's most rugged and remote mountain ranges on my own was daunting. Despite the challenge, I knew that being alone would afford me the opportunity to fully experience what I love most about being in the wilderness: the independence, the escape, the solitude. As a lone visitor I looked forward to focusing purely on the environment around me without distraction.

Titcomb Basin was the first destination on my multi-day trip. I had carefully detailed my intended route during the weeks prior to my journey, but upon seeing this cirque of magnificent granite peaks, I abandoned my intended itinerary to have an entire day to explore Titcomb Basin. I spent the day enjoying my freedom, scrambling up rocks for the best views, dipping my toes in the icy waters of crystal-clear alpine lakes and sketching the scenery from windy hilltops. For me, being in the outdoors is revitalising, rejuvenating, and inspirational. I can't help but feel that the mountains hold some kind of innate power. The gravity of their beauty and grandeur pulls me in and ignites my desire to explore and discover. During my journeys I find a deeper connection between myself and the majesty of these wild places.

Cerro Torre
CAROLINE EUSTACE

A childhood in suburban London through the 1950s and 1960s was all about climbing the apple tree in the back garden and roller skating up and down the uneven paving stones of Chestnut Avenue; but there was also adventure in our household.

My mother had been a local mountain guide in Snowdonia in the 1930s. There is a photo of her in a long skirt and plimsolls – she looks impressive, and my father, who was on holiday from London, obviously thought so too.

We only had one holiday a year, but it was all about fearless exploration of the UK: mountains, lakes, surf. It was also about enduring bad weather and packet soup. However, we did have three camping holidays abroad. These marathon drives around Europe sowed the seeds of travel-adventure in me. I discovered there was sunny weather and exotic food, and I too became relatively fearless.

The year 1970 – aged nineteen – saw me working in a mission hospital in Nquthu, Zululand, KwaZulu-Natal, before gap years were invented. That was enough to show me ways to move through this amazing world – especially enjoying the challenge of climbing as high as possible, whether it was up a mountain, a tower or a tree.

This is my drawing of Cerro Torre in Argentina. It was near the beginning of a two-month journey in 2014, following the Andes from Tierra del Fuego to the Bolivian border on public transport. My sketchbooks filled up with drawings of mountains, as well as of the plants and ants at my feet.

My excitement at being among mountains continues into my sixties. These days, just being there is enthralling enough and my sketchbooks record this. The paths are shorter and it's about the looking, the gentle breathing, and the pleasure of watching and responding to the world moving round me, rather than about the distance and the summit.

Mountain-Guide Dog

TAMI KNIGHT

Before I was born, my parents owned a dog that would ride the chairlift with them when skiing. As a kid, that dog's successor swam contentedly after us as we rowed in the dinghy. As a teenager, a third dog was a constant companion out hiking. Dogs, in my family, were always one-for-one members.

So, I get it that people love dogs. Now, I'm a cat person, but I would never dress my cat up as a mountain guide because it would wait till we got home and then shit on my pillow. A dog you can dress up, but a cat will retaliate.

She Collects Wild Islands in the Wild Wild Sea

PAULA FLACH

This piece is inspired by my friend Inger. She is a lovely and smart Norwegian lady with a passion for colours, IT and wild islands. To me the idea of an island is always exciting – a remote but brave little world unto itself amidst the sea. I'm sure this is the typical romantic bias of someone from a landlocked part of the world. The most popular book in my family was, is and will always be the atlas. Looking at these tiny green oddly shaped spots on the map always made me wonder what they look like in reality, what made people settle there and what geological miracle shaped them the way they are today.

Where does it hurt?
Carlos speaks Spanish, buys me
blister packs, pastries.

We pass my phrase book.
Like an angel, he buys dinner,
points to the word *gift*.

An old man's long shadow
on a church porch as I fill
my water bottle.

Each stone, shell, arrow
pointing the way is comfort;
haze of mountain snow.

Tables of pilgrims:
six languages with coffee,
comparing sunburn.

The steep path meets
mountain air, melting snow
and rim of sunset.

A wheelbarrow climbs
to the flags of Manjarín,
swishing with water.

Snapshots from the Camino de Santiago
CATH DRAKE

HEART of SOUL

Knees go hard downhill
on loose stones. We stop and compare
bruised and blistered feet.

A man appears, says:
sanitary pads are the best
for blisters – here, take!

Finally, a stream's rush
under a Roman bridge. I imagine
ice on raw feet.

I ask for water.
Australian? Note for you –
left four days ago.

Pilgrims are long gone,
I nap until noon then peel
out of bed, sightsee.

Snapshots from the Camino de Santiago
CATH DRAKE

A Child in These Hills

SOLANA JOY

I was born in Alaska. I left when I was fifteen, which was roughly half my life ago. I've lived in a lot of places since then, so I don't feel I can rightly call myself an Alaskan any more. Still, when people ask where I'm originally from, I tell them, 'Alaska,' and they – as though I'd just told them that I had parasailed into the bank queue from a glacier – invariably reply, 'Alaska?!'

Their surprise, though amusing, is fair; there aren't that many of us, statistically, and those that hail from that far north often never leave. A few brave souls might trickle their way down the West Coast, but that's about it. Which, again, is fair: if you're used to Alaska, and love it, you'd be hard-pressed to feel comfortable anywhere else. I've travelled all over, from Death Valley to Darjeeling, and while I've seen many strange and beautiful landscapes, I've not seen anywhere like home. The climate and the sheer size of everything – the mountains, glaciers, animals, etc. – make almost everywhere else seem pretty tame, crowded, and/or warm in comparison.

Children tend to assume that whatever they're born to is normal. So I thought it was normal to have grizzly bears in the yard every summer, and moose wandering through all year round. I thought it was normal to have to practise surviving avalanches, hypothermia and bear attacks at school. I thought the default dog breed was husky. I thought that everyone had to learn how to fish, pan for gold and ski.

I loved being an Alaskan … but I wasn't sure if I was very good at it. I wanted to build forts and snowmen, play capture the flag, and go skating like the other kids. But I seemed to be the only one afraid of the black diamond slopes that our parents started shoving us down in preschool. I was the last of my friends to get my training wheels taken off my bike. My hands and feet turned blue in the winter. Every form of transport made me instantly and violently motion sick. And I had recurring nightmares about falling off of mountains and ski lifts.

I didn't want to race through the rainforest! I wanted to go at my own pace, quietly, and see the flora and fauna lurking just beyond the path – the wild flowers and cubs that everyone zoomed past. I loved my beautiful homeland very much, and didn't understand why it wasn't enough to be in it – why did we have to go out and conquer it?

I was often shamed for my relative lack of speed or bravery, and my inability to keep up with the pack. And so, at fifteen, when my parents moved the family to Los Angeles, I was glad to go somewhere new. I figured I could run away from the embarrassment, start over, find somewhere I would really fit in. When I saw my new classmates driving to school in Hummers though, I realised I was going to be more out of place than ever. So I continued to look for somewhere to fit. I tried suburbs, small towns and metropolises across the US and EU. I sought camaraderie in universities, clubs, pubs and offices. I failed to thrive or even feel secure in any kind of social setting. I moved from place to place, chased professional and romantic leads that I knew weren't in my best interest, and misplaced friends like gloves along the way.

After about a decade of this, I began to despair; there must be something horribly wrong with me. I would look inside, and see nothing. I was like a tornado, throwing myself this way and that, making messes, moving on; a noisy outside with a hollow core. I wasn't beautiful, or brilliant, or talented, or even likeable. I had nothing to offer, and nothing to show for myself. No vocation, passion, dreams, resources or love. I was just a void. No, worse: a useless burden.

I was wrong to think I could get happy by running from problems that were inside of me. However, I wasn't wrong to run. I just needed to learn to run away from people altogether, rather than towards new ones.

I now advocate that everyone try this. You don't have to run far. I would love to complete an epic trek like Cheryl Strayed, or visit my grand Alaskan homeland. Risking life and limb out in the fiercely wild places is a wonderful thing – but isn't always viable, for health or money or other logistical reasons. And it isn't necessary. It turns out gentler landscapes can do the job just fine.

A few summers back I went on a 'find myself or die trying' kind of quest. I spent ten days at the Edinburgh Fringe, and was thoroughly exhausted with humans, with their need for both spectacle and attention. Their posturing, hollering and vomiting in the street. So I headed south to the well-grazed and much-praised Lake District.

The Lake District is *beautiful*, but not the wildest of the wild lands. Ever the bookworm, my interest in it was as much for its poets as the actual terrain they wrote about. It's been settled for ages – there's an ancient stone circle and everything. There are tourists and motorways, and little villages with only a few pubs and shops apiece. The only animals you're likely to encounter on the trail are ecstatic dogs and indifferent sheep.

So, no, it isn't an outrageously wild place; but it was bucolic as fuck. Nothing but rolling hills, fields, woodlands, streams and – of course – lakes. And then the sea beyond. I walked, and walked, and walked, and still only saw a sliver of it. I had very brief but amiable chats with other walkers – mainly couples, often retirees, trudging along in their waterproof jackets, orbited by collies and spaniels. I took pictures of quaint structures and exquisite butterflies. I wrote in my journal. I saw Dove Cottage, Wordsworth's grave and the world's only pencil museum. I bought tiny volumes of poems and cake recipes. I wore the same boots and trousers every day, and was perpetually windblown and scruffy. I had huge breakfasts at my B&B, ate apples and oatcakes and sweaty bits of cheddar along the trails, and devoured veggie stews in the pubs at night.

I had lots of time alone with my thoughts on these rambles, yet felt strangely detached from the worries that usually swarmed my conscience: career, cash flow, current events, correspondence, complexion and cellulite were concerns for humans elsewhere, in other lands. There wasn't much I could do about anything, anywhere, or for anyone, from up on a windy hill. The only important things there were heat, hydration, food, good socks and how soon the sun would set. I felt open and present and calm. I'd arrived in that strange, semi-mythical place called 'the moment'. And it felt divine.

After only a couple of days in this idyllic state, something extraordinary happened. I was standing beside Grasmere lake, just a short jaunt south of Dove Cottage. I stopped to lean against a chest-high stone wall along the water's edge and watched the sunlight ripple across. I laid my journal out on the wall, and wrote:

> 'I feel more myself than I have in ages. Or, at least, I was very conscious of the thought, "I feel like myself", which isn't one I have very strongly very often. A landscape of trees and water and clouds, a road and a general direction, a pack and a snack, sensible boots with nothing to do except start walking. Light in my eyes, tunes in my head, love in my heart. I feel more like joy, and more like Joy, than I can recall feeling so simply in ages. I feel very much to be that same wee Alaskan girl, clamouring through the leaves, as if she were still in me, unaltered by this quarter century that's passed … '

Suddenly, I saw the girl I was remembering. Not just remembered, but *saw* her. There was a version of myself, from a quarter-century prior, standing in the puddles along a gravelly lane through my home town. She was tiny inside a too-big, hand-me-down raincoat. She was peeping out from under her hood and fringe, smiling up at me. She was standing there, in Girdwood, Alaska, in the late 1980s, but somehow also in Grasmere, UK, in 2014.

If you were to look at that journal page now, you would see blotches from where I abruptly burst into tears at the sight of her. Or me. Little me. The me from when I last remember liking myself. That funny little girl who was always tramping about the woods with dogs. The girl who was constantly making up games, building forts, painting, tumbling, baking, writing and reading, reading, reading. Who didn't worry about the past, because she had none, and didn't worry about the future, because of course it would be brilliant. Because she knew that she was brilliant.

Tears of real, pure love and tremendous relief splashed everywhere. It must have been similar to the overwhelming relief of finding a lost child; which of course is what it was – just an inner child, instead of a borne one. My body was still leaning against the stone wall, but in my mind I very clearly saw myself reaching out and down, and giving this wee inner me a huge hug.

Eventually, the moment passed, and I got back on the trail. But I only went a short way before I had to stop again. Still overwhelmed by my vision, I sat down on the grassy ground in Penny Rock Wood, and wrote:

'I think, I hope, that we shall be one again, that there will
be no doubting our unity, our oneness, going forward.
I forsook her so often in the past, only to find that I cannot
live without her … She is most of what's best of me,
still – impish and open and fragile as she may be.'

✳ ✴ ✳

Shortly after I found myself, I also found a soulmate, who lives in Berlin. And now I live in Berlin, too. It's a serious metropolis: noisy, smelly, packed with construction crews and stag dos. I frequently have to fight an intense impulse to flee to somewhere green and pretty and calm; to try and get back to that feeling of myselfness that I found by Grasmere. But I am trying to teach myself to harness that feeling anywhere. I often stop and sit down: at my desk, or on a park bench, or wherever. I close my eyes and remind myself how it felt to be open and unencumbered along the trails, the smell and sound of the wind through the foliage, and I remember the expression of my inner child.

I remember, and I do feel better. Because now I know that I am not hollow, that I am not nothing; there is someone at the core of me. I have seen her. And I love her enormously. And it is my job to take the best care of her that I possibly can. It is easier to see her in the green places where she feels at home, but she is always with me just the same. She is not lost.

So the moral of the story is this: if you find yourself struggling, if you feel like you'll never find a way forward or a place to fit in, the only thing for it is to get yourself away. Just get the hell away from everyone that you can. Even the people you love. It doesn't have to be the ends of the earth, just away from the urbane. Don't wait for the perfect time. Walk out into mud, ice, bog, snow or sand – whatever you can manage. High-heeled humanity literally cannot follow you, and free from its filters you might find something truly precious: yourself.

Rewilding

LEE CRAIGIE

The usual parameters no longer exist.

There was a time when my arms stopped and the handlebars of my bike began, but not now. There was a time when the skin of my upturned face once prickled with the heat of the sun. Not now, now my face *is* the sun and behind what was skin there hisses and cracks enough energy to keep the world turning. My lungs and legs continue to move in and out and up and down like the bellows and pistons of a steam train, only now they do so effortlessly because they are no longer inhibited by the pain and discomfort my mind used to tell them they were experiencing. Their tussle with gravity and the elements has ceased. Everything is quiet and calm behind where my eyes used to be. I'm floating and free in this bubble of damp dirt and fresh sweat.

It's late May in the Scottish Highlands. Hopeful buds on trees are cautiously committing to the season ahead and shy ferns are now lengthening their spines in salutation to the unseasonably warm sun. It's day three of the Highland Trail, a 550-mile self-supported mountain-bike time trial around Scotland's most rugged and remote wilderness. I've slept under the stars for a total of six hours in the past fifty-five, and I've ridden, pushed or carried my bike over mountains and moorland in the blazing sun and the pouring rain for the rest of that time. Somewhere in the rational part of my semi-functioning brain I know that my body is exhausted and my clothing and equipment dirty and torn, but my normal functioning systems have shut down. I no longer feel sleepy or hungry. I feel no compulsion to wipe at the sweat falling into my eyes or to wash the caked mud from the exposed skin on my legs and arms. I am a wild beast, a feral and free form floating through my natural habitat. I no longer cease at the edge of it and have to force my fragile form into some alien shape that requires waterproofs and sun cream to survive in it. I have given myself up and feel strangely, euphorically, liberated.

People ask, 'Why race through these wild places? Why deprive yourself of sleep and food and the time to stop and appreciate where you are?' They tell me: 'You must miss so much moving like that!' and 'That's disrespectful of the natural environment you're moving through.' All that is true. Before reaching this feral equilibrium with nature, racing through the mountains on my bike as fast as possible is utterly self-absorbing and completely introspective. My only selfish concern is how well my body is moving over the inhospitable terrain; the landscape is an enemy that I must tame if I'm to continue to move productively through it. Disrespectful indeed.

But wait. Give it one more sunset and another sunrise. Strip it back. Pare it down. Underneath all that narcissistic centre-of-the-earth arrogance found in the bike racer lies another rhythm. Tucked below the cardiovascular and musculoskeletal systems there's a buzz and a hum that comes from deep, deep down, possibly even far, far back in the history of our genetic make-up. Hard to access on a daily basis when the comforts of modern-day living insulate us from it so effectively, but listen … be quiet: it is right there.

In the middle of an extended wilderness immersion this state is relatively easy to access, but occasionally, even amid the chaos of our concrete world rigged with wires and synthetic fibres, it's possible to hear the whisper from inside or perhaps far back in time. In these catalytic moments it's possible to feel the colour brown instead of smelling that newly dug flowerbed, or embody green when the rising sap of a young birch tree reaches out. In this world driven by thinking and doing, it's possible to forget just to be. Is 'just being' selfish? Is introspection indulgent? Do we need to drive and do and achieve to be considered worthy of the air we breathe? Or is letting go of our tightly held sense of self to merge with something bigger the most generous gesture we can make as humans. Human beings. Not human doings.

We are all unique, but each of us has the capacity to a greater or lesser extent to feel instead of think. To relinquish control and roll around in the dirt, to scoop food into our mouths with dirty paws and to sniff the air to gather information. We can draw strength from the sun and moon and survive comfortably on so much less than we think we can. Of course, this state can be experienced without the need for a period of sleep deprivation and intense physical depletion beforehand. But I am a creature of extremes. I will return to the earth intensely and with my whole heart only a couple of times a year, and to do so I have to work physically hard to escape the shackles of an everyday, mundane existence. When I feel them loosening, it's so exciting that I want to cry out. Howl, even. I'll keep pushing until my skin, tongue, ears and eyes can't bear the staggering amount of information being thrown at them any longer. I'll find myself vibrating from the yellow gorse, my eyes stinging with its potency, my nose filled uncomfortably with its pungent coconut smell and then … calm. I break the surface of the water and I'm on the inside looking out. My body ceases to hurt. My awareness of self slips away and I melt into the moss and the mud with exquisite relief. My moment, but universal.

Squamish

JEN RANDALL

We continued leaping into water when we moved to
Squamish, Canada. Moving so far from home was exciting
and traumatic, something we'd been planning for years
but couldn't really prepare for. Swimming and playing in the
water is a good way to forget – forget that you're far from
home, that you're starting again. Moving here marked the
first time in our nine years together that we were somewhere
we intended to stay, which is why this moment of Al landing
in the water is important. We had taken the leap and landed,
now for life to unfold.

Leaving for the Edge of the World
KATHLEEN JONES

*'Wild is a word like "soul". Such a thing may not exist,
but we want it, and we know what we mean when we
talk about it.'* – KATHLEEN JAMIE

The sun is shining as I leave Cumbria in mid May. The trees
are just coming into leaf and there are lambs in the fields.
The Lakeland fells on one side, and the Pennines on the
other, have shadings of white where wintry showers have
fallen overnight. Big puffs of cloud are being driven across
the blue sky by a cold northwesterly wind.

From the train I can see the stone walls that divide the
landscape, marking out old fields scattered with erratic
boulders left behind by Ice Age glaciers. I wonder what it will
all look like in four weeks' time when I come back.

If I come back.

This thought stops my breath for a moment. So many
things could happen. But I always have these moments of
anxiety when I go away. Travelling is a risk, going alone even
more so, but sometimes it's the only way to travel.

As a third-generation immigrant to England, I feel that,
if I belong anywhere, it's here. Although I've lived all over
the world at various times in my life, I've always felt myself
in exile when living anywhere other than Cumbria. But,
it seems as though I was born to be a nomad. There's an
English nursery rhyme that predicts your future according
to the day on which you were born, in lines that were often
quoted to me when I was a child.

*Wednesday's child is full of woe,
Thursday's child has far to go.*

I was born on a Thursday in a small farmworker's cottage in a hamlet too small to be visible on a map. Eden is on my birth certificate – the Eden river valley – a small paradise in a wild landscape. When I was three my father moved us up to the Scottish Borders to live on a croft in a place so wild there was no road to it. The front and back doors opened straight out on to the fellside, and cows and horses were stabled next to the living accommodation. There was no electricity or telephone; water came from a spring and the only toilet was an earth closet.

My parents were 'offcomers': my mother a land girl displaced by the war; my father the child of an Irish immigrant family, mill workers, cattle drovers and small farmers, displaced by poverty. He loved the land, loved farming, but couldn't afford to buy his own farm. So he laboured for another landowner in return for the croft. The people who wrenched a living from the land around us belonged to that land as my parents never could. They all traced their ancestry – and their language – back a thousand years to the Vikings who had settled there.

Most people over fifty had never been further than the nearest small town in their entire lives and many of them could read or write little more than their names. Having no electricity, there was no television to fill the evenings. People walked to each other's houses and had 'good crack'. As they talked, they peopled the landscape around me with stories. Old Sworley who had hanged himself in the barn believing that he had killed his wife by pitching her down the well (though she had actually survived). The woman whose ghost was supposed to walk the track on winter nights where her children had been lost in a snowstorm. How people had burned their furniture to keep warm through the winter of 1947. How Billy the Hope had spent three days floundering through the snow with a horse and sledge to fetch the supplies for his starving family. His story, as they told it, was a tale worthy of a Greek epic.

And on those fireside nights I learned my own family stories as I listened to my father and grandfather talking about ancestors who went across the sea on ships to bring back cargoes of bananas and marry exotic women; of others who drove herds of cattle from Ireland to London, or despaired over errant children, disinherited their offspring and fought bitterly over religion. These were stories they had learned from their own grandparents. I was aware, even at nine or ten, that I was listening to an unbroken memory line going back 200 years – stories passing like heirlooms from one generation to another. The tellers seemed to know exactly what great-great-grandmother Bridie had said to her daughter Frances Theresa when she came home with a baby she wasn't supposed to have, fathered by a footman at the house where she was in service. The fine rooms, the uniforms, the very porcelain crockery she washed in a lead-lined sink were all there in the story, leaping like a hologram in the firelight before my eyes. The account of my great-great-uncle Edward who had stood preaching the gospel of temperance outside his father's pub on a Tyneside quay, was pure Catherine Cookson. It was hardly surprising that I grew up with a love of history, language and narrative that was somehow equated with the wild, untamed landscape beyond the kitchen door.

Now, I live on the banks of the River Eden, not far upstream from the place where I was born, in an old mill perched on the bank of the river where it enters a natural gorge between sandstone cliffs. I can watch the river's variations through my window as I write: the delicate patterns of light and shade, the constant changes of mood. The murmur of the weir provides a continuing soundscape through every night and day. I know the riverbank intimately.

When I wake in the morning I can watch herons disputing territory above the weir, red squirrels bolting across the footbridge, spawning salmon in the gravel beds. Once, on a deserted morning, a family of three otters walked along the foot of the weir, and once we surprised a bird of prey lifting a duckling off the water. The river is a source of continuing fascination and delight.

So why am I leaving my own little paradise to travel to the edge of the world?

It all began with a growing disillusionment with Western politics and particularly with the West's attitude to environmental issues. There has, for a long time now, been a hollow, anxious feeling at the pit of my stomach. The news, both environmental and economic, makes me sad and frustrated because I care deeply about the state of the world we live in but I don't seem able to do anything about it. What will the future hold for my children, or my lovely grandchildren growing up so optimistically in a world that should be full of promise, but which now feels quite the opposite?

In the Mediterranean and the Andaman seas, refugees and asylum seekers are drowning in their thousands as they are turned away by affluent countries who could well afford to help. All over the world, big corporations are turning sections of the land and the ocean into wastelands that are too polluted to be safe. There are very few places in the world that man has not tampered with, and these days we do it by remote control – polluting an atmosphere and ocean that have no boundaries. The results are more than just environmental. Climate change and economic instability cause conflict. Some of the poorest countries are at war with each other, creating a living hell for the people who have to live there. In our own society, inequality is increasing at an alarming rate, fuelled by the austerity measures adopted by our governments as an answer to the banking crisis. As one economist put it, the result has been that 'money is being transferred from the have-nots to the have-yachts'. Long term, this too can only lead to conflict.

Then, in the autumn of 2014, I flew to Singapore and was horrified to be greeted at the airport by a notice exhorting all pregnant women, the elderly and people with breathing difficulties to stay inside with their windows and doors tightly shut because air pollution had reached a critical level. The city was hidden under a brown smog. You could see across the street, but only just. I thought that at least this must be some kind of environmental crisis, but no, people told me, this happens often. You have to stay inside. If you go outside you'd better wear a mask. Everyone behaved as if this was quite normal, and I found it unsettling. Singapore's neighbour, China, also has this problem on a daily basis.

The production of goods, power, drugs and chemicals that is required in our daily lives is damaging our environment, yet we seem unable to see a way out of the loop because we need the employment they provide in order to live and we want the goods that are produced. In the war between the environment and economics, economics definitely seems to be winning out.

But this situation, bad as it is, isn't the whole story behind my depression.

I write for a living, and inside myself there was a creative restlessness and dissatisfaction with an increasingly stale European literary tradition. Everything in poetry and prose seemed to have already been written. My connection with the natural world around me seemed also to have been broken. The girl who had run barefoot on the open fells among the larks and the curlews had vanished and the spontaneous joy she felt at being part of this wild landscape had long since been crushed under tax returns, deadlines, student reports, blog posts and bank statements. I felt flat, exhausted, despairing and powerless.

Then, at my lowest moment, I found a book by a Canadian poet, Robert Bringhurst, called *A Story as Sharp as a Knife*. It told the story of a group of First Nation people who inhabited remote islands off the northern coast of British Columbia and had a literary and artistic tradition reaching back more than 10,000 years. Their world view was, like most First Nation traditions, holistic, seeing human beings as part of the whole cycle of life on earth – part of an organism – a fragile ecosystem that commanded the utmost respect. Their world, which emerged after a great flood, was created – pulled up out of the water – by the Raven, who discovered human beings hiding in a giant clamshell and, thinking that he could have some fun with them, tempted them out.

The more I read of their myths and legends, the more I wanted to go. I dreamed of standing on North Beach, a spit of land where you can look straight out across the Pacific, where the Raven found the clamshell. I wanted to go somewhere truly wild, where the echoes of some of those first narratives still lingered.

So that is why I'm on a plane, at 38,000 feet, enduring all the discomforts of long-haul travel to visit a group of islands off the north-western coast of British Columbia and Alaska called Haida Gwaii. I don't know what will happen, or what difference it will make to my life; I just know that I have to do it.

[This is an excerpt from a travel journal of my journey to Haida Gwaii – *Travelling to the Edge of the World*.]

This Ocean Sings

DR ALEXANDRA LEWIS

This coast helps me breathe. It is a forceful lesson: nature's tough love. The salty air shakes and pummels me. Looking down the sheer drop my mouth parts as if to speak for the first time and the gust enters my lungs with a new urgency, pushing me back. The layers of sandstone tell of deep memory: its glinting ochre ribbons wrapping the coastline. Beyond that, the swash on rock, lone gulls riding the buffeting wind, a vast and endless sea. I am in the grip of land, water and sky.

I'd begun the day in the national park, looking for the path to Redhead Beach. I'd tried before and been diverted, led around the brackish edge of the lagoon and emerging disoriented in playing fields not far from where I'd started. A circle where I'd wanted a line. A second attempt uncovered a different track leading to the same bemusing conclusion. Did the way not want to be found? How hard could it be to follow a straight line, through coastal heath and forest, tinged with the scent of wildflower, heading south?

You enter the Awabakal Nature Reserve from the top of Knoll Avenue or Ocean Street, passing the shell of housing developments with their pricey ocean glimpses. The whistling and chatter of workmen will stay with you till the gravel road thins out and reaches its cul-de-sac. The leaf litter underfoot is mulchy after overnight rain; each step releases a crisp scent and a scurrying of ants and beetles. A few minutes further and the loudest of the calls dies away. There is the shock of sudden silence, and after a momentary deafness the secondary realisation that your ears are adjusting to a discreet orchestra of sound. Foremost is the rustling of leaves overhead. There are bellbirds, offering up their note with

piercing certainty. The movement of the dappled light is so
powerful as to almost throw out a noise all its own. You are
out of the brute force of the sun now and the sweat whispers
a trail down your temple, promising to diminish but not
quite carrying through.

At first the trail is wide and inviting. Sand and dirt mingle.
You might walk here in company, three abreast. You can see
all around you. This land was first home to Awabakal family
groups, whose traditional territory spreads from Wollombi
to the Lower Hunter. In 1978 the government declared this
area part of a conservation corridor; precious wilderness
protected between suburbs and sea. You will pass into a
clearing, a meeting space, where you find discarded cans,
the remnants of a small fire, and in the very centre a
towering and aged tree. A modern bench. Paths sweep away
in three directions. A trick of the topography means you may
hear wafts from the builders' radio – echoes from another
place. With an involuntary shiver you shuffle through onto
the leftmost path, glad as it rises towards a final ring of
stones with unobstructed views of the ocean. Redhead Beach
can be seen from here. Doubling back, the track – I now
know – can be found to the left. You'd need to push through
dense scrub at the most imperceptible of openings. Sharp
branches would urge you back, whipping at arms and face
as you pass. Overgrown is putting it mildly. Visibility is low,
and with the flies buzzing and your blood thrumming there
is every chance you might smack bang into another walker
before you'd seen or heard them coming.

But if you didn't spot the track to Redhead Beach, you
might continue on the second path out from the clearing,
as I did, always heading left when faced with further
divisions, sticking (or so you think) close to the line of the
coast. The ground underfoot is firmer, less sandy now, and
the path here too becomes thin, though passable. Your eyes

are drawn by large roots and twigs that reel back like snakes as your trainers come down, one after the other, a mesmeric visual pattern, till you realise with a start you've no idea what's around you at arm's reach. Pause a moment to catch your breath. Lean on a scribbly gum and trace the delicate patterns across its smooth bark.

It's hard to pinpoint the moment at which I started to feel uncomfortable. It happened each time I passed this way. Initially, distracted by insteps aching with the effort of a swift descent, I realised my heart was beating me a message of fear. I pause to flick a small grass burr from the edge of my sock, taking in the changed air and odour of the lagoon nearby. Earlier on, the track was peaceful. Here it doesn't feel right, and I catch myself looking over my shoulder and into the bush, scanning for eyes, or faces. I do this repeatedly, though don't know how I'd react if I saw someone lunging towards me. I quicken the pace, sheepish, but it's true that the kookaburras are laughing cruelly in this gully and it rings in my ears like a warning.

Something about this place imposes itself upon me. I shudder to think about life for the Awabakal people when white men first invaded this, their territory.

My legs shake with vulnerability. In a flash I remember the glinting knife that threatened me outside a tube station on the other side of the world. This ground is well charted, I tell myself. From that lagoon the helicopter buckets drink their fill in fire season. There are houses not too far from here. I break into a trot. A jogger comes towards me and I am relieved to take in his branded sportsgear, headphones and pained smile.

It is in the playing fields, back in mobile reception, that I search for a map of the trail I'd missed and find instead articles about the Awabakal *crime scene. Hearts sink as body is found.* Police had *scoured dense bushland.* Just *a few kilometres from the sixteen-year-old's home.* Rescue crews *abseiled down a cliff face and recovered the badly decomposed remains after noticing an unusual smell.* Officers have since revealed that *they are not treating the death as suspicious.* But *family had said her disappearance was completely out of character. It is understood that nail polish was found on the body.* One month ago.

So I head back via the streets of Dudley and into the Glenrock State Conservation Area. Here I am untroubled by the eerie feeling, yet the dead girl remains in my mind. On some of these tracks there is only one way in and one way out. I make for the open space of the beach, for the howl and yelp of the sea.

T.S. Eliot wrote of the sea having many gods and voices, but perhaps Thoreau was right in thinking that, *generally speaking, a howling wilderness does not howl: it is the imagination of the traveller that does the howling.* If you need to scream into the sea: on a good day, the winds will carry the troubles away from your mouth and disperse them; on a bad day, they might be flung back in your face. At least, either way, you have placed them outside of yourself.

Here on the sand I find tracks of dogs and horses, men and women, the scuttle prints of crabs and a small ray washed up and awaiting the tide. I bare my feet and keep walking. Soon there is only me and the sand ahead is unwritten. Every so often a group of blue stingers, sacks of air glistening in the sun, lie with poisonous filaments stretched over the wet surface like an artwork. These splashes of colour leave hardly any mark on the textured canvas beneath them. I imagine them floating mindlessly in tides, taut bottles cresting the waves as the drooping tentacles perform their underwater ballet, wrapping the phantom spaces where an arm, leg or fin might be found.

The deep blue of the sky joins the full ocean. The spray surrounds me. My mind is clear and ready.

Here on the east coast of Australia, doors to the wild self spring open. I keep walking north, unfurling to the elements. My love for the landscape is a hunger. There are stories here, patterns in the rock, imprints from the Dreaming; but they are not mine to tell. With my hands and my feet and my eyes I listen, with my body I strain to understand.

On the clifftop, a clarity. I store this feeling up for inside buildings, at desks, by televisions, stopped in queues.

Returning to the house I happen upon a man from the neighbourhood. We know each other by nods rather than names. He crosses the road and I kneel to pat his dog and the heads of the other dogs he is walking. There are so many dogs to greet that conversation between humans seems inevitable. He used to cycle the Redhead track as a kid, he tells me, though he agrees it is too overgrown these days to walk alone. He grins and scratches at his beard. As we talk the smell of fresh bread from the bakery nearby rises above the salt and the sweat of the passing day. Neither of us mention the missing local girl. We wave goodbye.

I look back towards the ocean and hear it sing.

To Follow

CLAIRE CARTER

Remembering I wondered if I moved first
or if you touched me
did it seem like I had been waiting

you placed this rock in my hand
and closed my fingertips over it

softly unclothed
where your hollow has grown cold
I wake and wake again
into dark
fingering the creases in the sheets
lost in folds of cloth without a map
or patterned alignment
of tors or stars
to landmark the bed

street lamps cleave from the trees at dawn

the evening dregs stiffen on the table
as I make to leave

I have been sent out to follow you

if you see something
anything
reach out, touch wood
mark the moss

bend the bracken aside in places
press your hands into the peat
lie down in the sand
leave footprints well away from the waves

high above wide lands
the path runs
along broken limestone ridges
and descends between clefts
and downy pines

at times I find yarn leading from
still tarns
and cairns built on flat ground

in these days the wind
has been known to file the sky
to thin blade
did you ever watch the lightening crawl
like a broken man across the cliffs

two hundred feet above the waves
I crawl along a black zawn
seabirds scream and spit
they pause mid flight
as if they would choose to fall
I watch silently
as their bodies plummet past
to rip apart with sudden wings in the spray

the light is turning
previously blank rock jostles with minerals in the gold
elements of driftwood, glass and bone converse with the shingle
learning the shape of the sea
until dark

when crouched boulders wash their secret parts in salt water

I head inland
a gullet in the ground
has swallowed the way

no fenland glimmering in the mist but
the flint lips of a newly
scoured maw
where the path has caved in

unmapped and in tatters
the track in my head unwinds
to its thread ends
they drift
and catch
in dead sea thrift

will you let yourself be lost

my hands are hatched
with such regular notches
I can count the days spent
following
lines split into the land
mottled, brackish knuckles crack
like rotting gulls eggs

as the dead's hair grows from bone
lichen beards our walls

but the door stutters on the latch

so I stay awake

and cycle back and forth through these days
slow without your slipstream

the trees are so simple now
they drift in the road

Cayton Bay

GENEVIEVE CARVER

I'd argued with myself the whole way there
not joining in with the B-movie script you all rehearsed
across me   the hot car constricting my innards
I climbed out of the rear window
and strapped myself to the roof with the surfboards
the 1960s pastiche we couldn't shake off
I stared up at the conflicted sky and waited for rain
to wash me on to the moss-tufted cliff
shrug me from its chalk-bald scalp and into
silk-grey tears as far as the eye can shed
feeling no more real than the bloodshot limestone wreck
squinting out over the gambling, sugar-scoffing town
the wellied walkers with their creatures   pointless
pointlessly I stared up at the conflicted sky and waited
for waves to rip the sickness from the pit of me
the melodrama I couldn't shake off
silk-grey tears as far as the eye can shed
I'd argued with myself the whole way there
and lost.

Leaving Protection

MARIA COFFEY

After all these years, the routine was automatic, like breathing. Pull on my waterproof jacket, sprayskirt and rubber boots. Zip up my life jacket and cinch it tight at the waist. Grab a paddle and lift the 50-pound kayak – first on to my knee then a quick hoist up to my shoulder. Negotiate a few rough steps to the beach. Trust my feet to instinctively find their way across rocks slippery with seaweed and sharp with barnacles. Drop the kayak into the water, sit into the cockpit, attach the skirt to its rim. Push off.

The air was sharp, fresh and briny. High clouds scudded by, the sun playing peekaboo behind them. In the shallows, a great blue heron stood stock-still staring into the water, her long neck feathers ruffled by the wind. As the kayak glided towards her she let out a prehistoric squawk, opened her huge wings and skimmed over the water to a neighbour's wooden dock. One of our cats had followed me. He sat on a rock, a big ball of black and white fur against the yellows and browns of the beach, meowing in protest as I paddled away.

'Go home, Teelo!' I called out.

Home was a small beachfront house on tiny Protection Island, off the coast of British Columbia. I had arrived here almost two decades before, reeling from a hurt and confused past. My lover, a British mountaineer, had been lost without trace near the summit of Everest. I was adrift, bouncing between projects and places, trying to make sense of life without him. I had planned to stay in British Columbia for a year, and then head to Australia. Six months in, I met Dag. He had just moved to Protection, a narrow scrap of land barely a mile long, just off big Vancouver Island

where I was teaching. He took me there in a rowing boat
on a snowy February day. He was crazy about the ocean;
he couldn't wait for the summer to go swimming, sailing
and kayaking. We were brand new; I didn't want to admit
to him straight away that I was hydrophobic, a committed
landlubber. Some years before, in Morocco, I had been
caught by a rip tide and carried out into rough waters.
By the time I was hauled ashore I had stopped breathing,
and was resuscitated on the beach. As Dag rowed across
the harbour raving about the ocean life, I clung to the
gunwales, tensing at every little wave.

During our first summer together, Dag helped me face
my fears, gently coaxing me to go swimming. At first I stayed
close to the shore, where I could stand up. Gradually I edged
into deeper waters. Small waves hitting my face brought
panic, with flashbacks of choking, my throat closing, my life
seeping away. It took time and patience but I grew confident
in the water. I would swim out, amazed at how far I was
from land. I would float on the surface staring up at passing
clouds, appreciating every precious breath.

By the second summer we were married and living in
a tiny rented cabin on the island. It was perched on a bluff –
steep steps cut into the rock led down to the shoreline. The
cabin had no running water, only a barrel in which to collect
rain, so we bathed in the sea. We swam first thing in the
morning, right after waking up, several more times during
the day and often at night. Ah, those night swims. It was
like sliding through silk. And all around our bodies were the
sparkling bursts of bioluminescence – I could see the outline
of Dag's shape, as if he was enveloped by stars, while I was
a watery Tinker Bell, in a cloud of pixie dust. To be in the dark
ocean without fear was a miracle in itself, but nothing had
prepared me for such astounding, transcendent beauty.

I steered the kayak into the channel between Protection and the island across from it, thinking about those swims during my first summers here. They got longer and longer, until eventually I could swim the 300 metres across the channel and then back again. It was the same with paddling. Dag had built us a couple of kayaks so that we could commute from the island to the nearest town, a mile away. At first my arms were so weak I would count the strokes and try to get up to twenty, to fifty, then to 100 without stopping. I could not have imagined that I would embark on long expeditions, paddling up to eight hours a day amid sharks in the Solomon Islands, past floating bodies along the Ganges River, and dodging hippos on Lake Malawi.

I looked back, and saw that Teelo had given up his protests. He was picking his way over the rocks, back to the piece of land that Dag and I bought during our third summer together, and the house we built on it. A small wooden house with soaring cathedral windows, embracing the view across the Georgia Strait to the snow-capped mainland mountains. Dag created a garden, and dug a pond that frogs moved into, singing their love songs each spring. He built me a little writing cabin. He built an outdoor sauna from which we plunged into the cold ocean and then sat steaming on the rocks. The house was a magnet for our friends. We threw parties that lasted for days, going kayaking and swimming, cooking up huge feasts and carousing into the early hours while our guests' children slept in the spare room, curled up around each other like kittens.

Time had passed. Those children were grown up. I had come to the island as a young woman; now I was middle-aged. And we were leaving. The property had sold and would change hands within a month. I couldn't imagine saying goodbye. The house, the view, the land and sea seemed like extensions of my being. Sitting at the kitchen table with

a purring cat on my lap, gazing across at the mountains –
after so many years this still gave me enormous pleasure,
and centred me. There were many sound reasons for why
it was time for us to leave, but the ache of impending
separation was deep.

I paddled out of the channel, along the north shore of
Protection and past the old cabin we had rented on the bluff.
The steps looked different now, eroded by wind and rain.
At the base, I recognised the big rock where, at the right
tides, I used to sit for hours. After we got married I had
to wait a few months for my immigration papers to come
through, and in the meantime I couldn't work. Each morning
after our swim and breakfast, I perched on that rock and
watched Dag paddle off to his job on Vancouver Island.
Then I sat, and took in my surroundings. The sucking
of barnacles. The crack of shells dropped by gulls on
to the rocks. The squeaky calls of eagles. The silver flash
of a jumping fish. Seaweed undulating in a current.
An approaching wind darkening the water's surface.
The creeping progression of the tide.

I had never lived by the sea before. Its moods and
rhythms were a revelation, and paying attention to them
brought visceral changes. My periods had always been crazily
irregular, but they began to arrive as if appointed, to the day
and almost to the hour. And my mind had calmed. I saw life
scrolling out ahead of me, full of possibilities. I looked back
at the territory I had crossed, at the questions and hurts left
unresolved by a sudden death, so painful that I had buried
and tried to forget them. I took a notebook down to the
rock, and I began to write. During those mornings by the sea
words came, at first hesitantly and then in a great cathartic
rush. I wrote my way my backwards, starting to untangle the
knots of the past, so that I could move into my future.

I sat in the kayak, remembering the younger me sitting there and scribbling. Tears ran down my cheeks and into the collar of my jacket; I was overwhelmed by the thought of leaving this island. It was where my love with Dag had blossomed. It was where I had become a writer. It had been the centre of everything, of all the happiness I'd known these past twenty years. It was an anchor that had allowed us to cast off and travel far, knowing we could always return. We embarked on madcap journeys: a year around the world with a folding kayak, three months cycling up the coast of Vietnam, a ten-week kayak circumnavigation of Vancouver Island. We barely finished one trip before we were planning another. But wherever we went, our island home was always in my mind – a strong thread of connection that I knew would pull us safely home.

Dag was away now in Europe, sorting out some family affairs. I had time on the island alone and I was grateful for that. For him, the leave-taking was going to be easier. Despite his deep attachments to this place he was ready for a change, and excited about what lay ahead for us. It was hard for him to see me upset and I knew he was worried about me falling apart when we moved. I was worried about that, too. I had a friend, with a strong spiritual bent, who had recently moved from a much-loved island home after thirty years. She had done so with equanimity and grace. I turned to her for advice.

'Collect some small beach stones,' she had said. 'Take them around the property. Recognise things, places, memories you are grateful for. Attach each one to a stone. Keep the stones somewhere you can see them while you're packing up.'

'And then?' I'd asked. 'What do I do with them?'

'Leave them behind. It's acknowledging the gratitude that counts. That will always stay with you.'

At first I had laughed. So New Age! So West Coast! But
the idea grew on me and began to make sense. And I knew
where I should gather my stones. Turning the kayak, I headed
out into the Georgia Strait. An easterly wind was starting to
blow and I leant into my paddle strokes, adjusting my course
towards the smudge of land two miles away.

Snake Island is tiny, uninhabited and shaped like a comma.
Along its northern shore are intricate sandstone galleries,
sculpted in flowing shapes and overhangs. Grassy meadows
cover the highest area, a nesting ground for seabirds. At the
far end is a navigation light and from here the mainland
mountains look huge, stretching right across the horizon.
A twin beach and sheltering rock outcrops are haul outs for
seals and sea lions. Close by, bald eagles perch on driftwood
snags. Dag and I felt incredibly lucky to have this wild piece of
land in our 'backyard'. We had paddled out here countless times
in every season, in all sorts of weather and sea conditions. Each
visit seemed special and meaningful. 'Going to Snake' was like
a pilgrimage, a renewal of our spirits and a reminder of what
mattered in life, of why we lived on this coast.

Halfway through the crossing, a few seals popped
their heads up, gazed at me with big liquid eyes, then slid
under the water again, their noses the last part of them to
disappear. As I approached Snake, I made out the bulky
shapes of more seals – over a hundred – lolling on the beach
and rocks bordering it. I had rarely seen so many there at
one time, and I was going to paddle by and circumnavigate
the island rather than disturb them. But one noticed me and
started moving, then the whole gang erupted, splashing into
the water and surfacing all around me, a host of slick heads
gleaming in the sunshine.

The beach was short and steep, and made of smooth
stones. At its high point was a familiar driftwood log, stout

and weathered silver, and I placed the kayak on top of it out of the tide's reach. Then I sat for a while, leaning back against the log, watching red-beaked oystercatchers running hectically through tide pools, calling to each other in shrill whistles. The seals were still milling around in the bay. When I stood up and headed towards the sandstone galleries, half of them followed me. They swam close to the shore, snorting loudly, gamboling, popping up to stare at me then submerging with big splashes. I sat under one of the overhangs and they gathered in a group right below me. I laughed in delight, yelled, 'Hello guys!' and the water frothed as they all dived from sight, only to re-emerge in seconds.

Climbing back to the top of the island, I walked through the long grasses, out to the light beacon and then back to the beach. So many memories flooded in. I smiled, remembering the time we paddled over to Snake as a huge full moon was rising, thinking it would be romantic to sleep on the beach. The gulls were confused by the brightness of the moon and flew around us all night, screeching in mad abandon. We finally drifted off, only to be woken by seals that had hauled up alongside our sleeping bags, snorting and farting. Eventually we gave up, and paddled home to our bed.

Shadows were lengthening, the wind was picking up and whitecaps flecked the surface of the water. I knew I should leave soon. I walked slowly along the beach, choosing small stones and filling my pockets with them. I knew I might never go back there. So I was surprised, as I pushed off in my kayak, to find myself calm, happy and suffused with gladness for all the times Dag and I had spent on this tiny piece of paradise.

Five seals accompanied me as I paddled away. This wasn't unusual – we'd often find seals swimming behind our kayaks. But these five swam ahead of me. They dived and I thought they were gone, then suddenly they surfaced, looking back as if to make sure I was there. I was paddling towards the sinking sun. Ahead lay little Protection, dwarfed by the silhouette of Vancouver Island behind it. The seals appeared again and again; I imagined they were leading me into my new life. And then they swam away, leaving me to paddle on alone. As I reached the beach outside our house the sun slipped below the horizon.

Our last summer on this island had waned. Sunshine left the garden earlier each day, spiders spun big webs between tree branches and the temperature was cooling. Dag would soon be home, and we'd make final preparations for the move.

I sat at the kitchen table with a cat on my lap. The stones were spread out before me, and I touched each one. I had followed my friend's advice. I'd carried the stones around the house, the garden, the beach, the island, attaching memories and gratitude to them. I realised that a big part of my fear about leaving had been that it might break some spell and shatter the membrane of happiness that surrounded me. But a root of that happiness was the deep connection to the ocean and to the earth that I had found here. It had opened me to the solace of nature. It had given me moments of the utmost joy. I had taken that connection around the world with me, and it had enhanced every one of my journeys. Once found – I now knew – it could not be lost.

Dag returned, and the serious packing began. On our last night, we had a sauna then sat at the water's edge. Dag talked about what we had given back to this place. We had gifted it with our love, joyfully swimming and kayaking in its waters and walking on the land, every single day. In our wake we were leaving beauty: an exquisite little house that blended into its environment, a natural garden and a happy spirit that the next owners had recognised the moment they first visited. 'We've honoured it,' said Dag. 'We couldn't have appreciated it more.'

The last few weeks had been golden, but now the first system of early autumn moved in, and I woke before dawn to hear rain hammering on the roof. A truck filled with our belongings was parked on the lane at the end of the garden, and we would drive it a short distance to the dock where a barge was waiting. There were just a few more things to load, including the cats in their carriers. Dag was watching me anxiously, anticipating a meltdown of tears. I told him I had to do one more thing, and I went back to the house alone. I quickly walked through it, saying goodbye. Then I stepped down to the beach, and reached into my pockets for the stones. I held them for a few seconds, took a deep breath then shouted 'Thank you!' flinging them into the air. I watched them arc skywards and splash into the water. For the last time I looked across to Snake Island, and to the mainland mountains, cloaked in clouds. My cheeks were wet with raindrops, but not with tears.

'There are a thousand ways to kneel and kiss the ground,' wrote Rumi. With a friend's help I had found my way. It allowed me to climb calmly into the truck, smile at Dag and say, 'Let's go'.

Running by the Quay in Exeter

EVELYN O'MALLEY

Once a joke, but never a runner. At primary school sports day, I focused so much on keeping the spud on the spoon, contemplating its plonky wobble, that I forgot to race at all. They finished up long before I made it to the line. I grew up to love wandering outside, but steered clear of running.

Then unexpectedly at thirty, a friend and I find ourselves living together in Exeter, adrift. At first, running is about bodies, not landscapes. Running on treadmills, occasionally outside – measuring changes.

Spring tempts us out with daffodils and blossoms, and the quay's cheaper than the gym. It's warmer too and no one's staring – or if they are, there are two of us – so more and more we're outside, running down to the quay, canal, the floodplain, up to the swing bridge, back through the cow field and by the river. Keeping to the paths.

Is that really an abattoir we can smell from the other side of the canal? Think gossamer, gossamer-light as we plod, taking turns singing, spotting nettles, allotment sunflowers, sheep, watching the weather come down over Haldon Hill. One plum tree from a stone discarded long ago. Nearer the M5, nearer the sea.

She moves north, in love. I stop running. But after a while my legs ache to move again, missing the route, our plodding through the seasons. So I venture out, the paths familiar – quay, canal, floodplain, swing bridge, cow field and river – but running with absence. It's different on your own.

I'm scared of the anorak with the quadcopter by the canal so go another way. Always keep a little energy back for the cow field. Harry says cows are more dangerous than sharks. I leave the headphones behind; my ears are too small and they just won't stay put. Also, you're never going to hear the dinosaurs coming if you have headphones in.

On rainy, quieter days, self-consciousness dissipates and I begin to notice, to love where I am. I'm splashing in puddles, wet grass leaky through my runners and there are rabbits and rats in the cow field too, and noisy, noisy insects I can't see through the swervy buttercup path. Flashes of a blue gingham dress in Oz on a Betamax with grandparents. Bitey flies are crunchy if you don't close your mouth. And can I know these trees if I don't know their names? And, oh, the surprise of the light, the mist, on the cathedral back behind. It was always here that I needed to be.

Song lyrics, an imaginary soundtrack, flit in and out, keeping pace. Acorn crunch. Snail crunch. Windy, wincey and slip-toe over the grate. Rachel Sermanni's singing in my head about waves that won't carry anyone and I remember that people are drowning on boats and the news said we're sending barbed wire to Calais so run, keep running, because what'll you do when you stop.

This is the bramble where Aoife, visiting, fell off her hire bike. A tactical dismount into the ditch. Invisibly Irish, still our bodies remember this landscape isn't ours. A raincoat covered the scratches but the indignity imprinted, left pressed into the hedgerow.

I'll come down with Mark to pick blackberries later. The easy-to-reach ones disappear quickly on the weekends but the highest-up ones get left for the birds. No one's hungry enough to get brambled.

A theatre company performed a play about wolves here last autumn, by the river where dogs are allowed to run free. I ran with Joe and a lady we met, chased by wolf-actors – just the three of us running through the woods in the dark. For just a little longer than felt right. Stars were out; their timing must've been out. Or maybe we were tired. Or maybe

I'm scared of the dark. We ended in the cow field, a trail
of bobbing head torches and a fiery circle for protection.
And I ran home by myself. Fast.

Accidently run through a spiderweb I didn't see. Probably
closest I'll come to a finish line, but I'm sorry for the spider.

Flies zoom, scatter from a dog poo; rabbits scram into the
hedgerow, scared of me.

I catch another woman's eye and she gets it too, maybe.
Something about bodies that isn't about gym bodies but
living ones today, outside on adventures, alone, despite and
with the world.

This landscape's brambles, cows, spiders, cyclists, seagulls
and weather. It's crumbly tarmac, rocky paths and secret
grassy traces of other runners who found better ways.
It's Aoife, Mark, Joe and the lady and Rachel Sermanni
and a clicky left foot. And our fears, the subtle shamings
tangled in the brambles and the breathing in the rain.
And I'm running with a kind of joy – salty, sweaty
heartclutch of alive – not very fast and not very far. Down
to the quay, canal, floodplain, swing bridge, cow field and
river to the road, further and further, and home, Exeter, love
for a friend who dragged me out, and a potato on a spoon
are marking out the distance.

Straggle

ALLISON WILLIAMS

God bless the straggler, working harder than anyone else on the mountain. We climb in a panic, but we are climbing harder than you. We operate at full capacity to keep up with others who moderate their speed out of pity or annoyance. We forsake the water stop in favour of pushing on and trying to catch up.

And as we the stragglers stumble up the last few steps on the rocky spine of a volcano to where the others have paused, watch how they nod and take off again; catching up is a momentary prize snatched out of the straggler's hands and tossed again up the mountain.

When that straggler is a woman, watch the back of her neck tighten with shame and determination, the refusal to let her gender be the excuse for anything. Watch her hate her own weakness even when it's the only part of herself she recognises. Because weakness isn't an attribute, not an appendage. It is us.

I used to take camping trips in Alaska, up the Eagle River valley in the Chugach just outside of Anchorage. In a wilderness the size of big dreams and epic adventure, this pocket of Alaska was practically suburban, a trailhead only a few miles from gas stations and pizza joints. But the Sitka spruce grew thick down the sides of the valley and the river churned white all summer long. Overhead a glacier melted into the shape of a polar bear pelt, draped over the triangle peaks like a bearskin rug. The bears wouldn't have cared that this wasn't the wildest of Alaska.

There wasn't much physical exertion on the trips, just a few miles down a well-trodden trail to a yurt perched above the river. Other friends would camp closer in, inside a claustrophobic cabin that filled with the smells of sleeping adults all night. I chose the yurt, with the boys.

The boys were not boys at all but grown men who used the summer camping trip to steal back parts of their boyhood selves. Not the carefree bounding of young boyhood, the glee at climbing over rocks and logs – the kind of boyhood I'd had too, as a little girl. This was the anxious, clubby boyhood of pre-adolescence, the joy of sneaking contraband and keeping others out of the tree fort.

They were suburban fathers and I was a city woman, but we were more than those few days. We were comrades, war buddies, a crew.

Keeping up meant trying the anachronistic tobacco pipes they showed off. This one was hand-carved from bone. This one was bought from the best pipe-maker in Los Angeles. Isn't this tobacco premium? Why don't people smoke any more? Why don't we do this more often?

I'm not the only girl, but I'm the only one that takes part, trying the feel of a pipe between my lips. I can't catch the rhythm, and kick the dirty air back out of my mouth before it even reaches my lungs. Play it down. Keep up.

The mosquitoes outside are monstrous, relentless, and so we stay inside the yurt next to a pot-bellied stove that could probably burn the yurt down. It's almost too hot to stay inside, but this is Alaska, where even the dead of summer is reasonable. The round space fills with tobacco smoke and it's not that I try not to show my discomfort – I deny that I feel it. I like this. I love this.

I call them 'the boys', these men, with an air that's half affection and half bemused mother hen. Inside jokes form in front of me and yet I still can't quite get inside them.

Once the whisky is opened I find the place I can keep up. I can do this kind of camping. The next day I don't so much have a hangover as I've simply lost the inside of my body. It's nothing but airy, empty space between the insides of my skin. Halfway to the privy I have to lie down in the dirt – not because the world is spinning but because there's absolutely nothing left inside to power my body forward. When I rise up from the forest ground I expect to be covered in sticks and mud, evidence of my inability to hold my liquor. But if I am, when I return to the yurt, no one has noticed.

We laugh and we drink more, our entire stay in the yurt one extended campfire circle of joviality. When I suggest a hike up the Eagle River valley, some of the boys come with me, but they do so with a shrug. I am trying. They are not, at least not until I shoot out ahead through Sitka spruce as brushy as pipe cleaners. The valley opens up and the sawtooth mountains above look like they know what they're doing.

Leading down the trail I stop feeling out of the loop and like my limbs have everything wrong. The trail follows the river, crossing tributary streams on fallen logs where my sneakers grasp the sandpaper bark for balance. Feet sink into the quicksand of gravel and glacial silt along the riverbank and I don't want to take pictures when we stop.

It finally feels like we did something. Back at the yurt, those who stayed back greet us with the barest of interest. One of the boys who'd followed me calls my hiking pace 'the Bataan Death March' and I laugh with the rest. 'Sorry,' I say. I am not too earnest.

The other half of our party – the ones at the cabin – have been hiking all over the valley, venturing up spidery animal trails and passing by the bogs dotted with moose. They stop by our yurt to tell us about the baby carriage they discovered halfway up the ridge; incongruous and eerie on a trail far too knotted with roots to be passable for a stroller. The story is quickly forgotten when they depart but I can't stop thinking about the mystery still wedged into the forest, the open question of just what happened to the baby. I wonder why I'm not out discovering the rest of the valley's secrets.

The tobacco, the whisky, the weed. We barely eat, too full to break into our foodstuffs, and I am on alert every moment for a break in conversation that I can enter. The boys laugh at my jokes and make jokes at my expense, complain about their lives, and tell me how to rip the wings off a ptarmigan you've hunted in the woods. Every minute I'm keyed in to the current I'm up against, pushed by a centrifuge to the outside of the circle, the fringe.

This is camping. The hooting jokes, the nasty stories about everyone we know in common, passing the bottle as the Alaska sun finally sets beyond the yurt's mesh windows. The boys stand in a row on the edge of the yurt deck to urinate into the bushes with a dramatic view of the valley, and for a moment I give my exhausted attention span a rest.

When they return I'm enveloped in their attention, in the inclusion. I find the right retort to the right joke; I tease the right person at the right time. We are adults, but we click into camaraderie in a way none of us has for decades – protected by concentric circles of forest that buffer us from our lives.

On the way back to the car, I detour into the woods at just the right moment, trusting an inner GPS that's always right. Years ago on my first trip to the valley I'd built a fort here among the moose droppings and spruce trees, a childlike lark with friends that no longer joined the summer outings. I can still find its remains, or at least the stone wall that had supported a roof of tree limbs. I can't believe the moose haven't trampled it, that the snows haven't completely collapsed the brickwork of rocks we made. I run my hands up the ruins with tears in my eyes, but I can't really say why I'm crying. I know why I didn't invite anyone else back to my ruins, though. It's not that they would laugh at me, it's that they'd shrug. I love my little ruin, but apparently that is no longer camping.

People go outdoors to push themselves past what they thought they could do … or at least that's what I keep hearing. If you keep engaging the engine of your body to its fullest potential, you reach the mountain not with gasps and tripping catch-up steps but with authority and with strength still thrumming through your body.

I go outdoors for the struggle, not to beat it. Because every time I beat it, I forget about it and it stops being something that hangs from my neck in shame. It winds its way around my muscles like spiderwebs, like lichen. Climbing a mountain isn't supposed to be easy, and maybe you're not even supposed to climb it. I'm a straggler up trails I can't quite climb because I don't know how to never start, and because it's never about the others I trail behind.

Falling

JOANNA CROSTON

It all happened
so quickly
a single inhalation
one moment climbing
then one crampon
catches the opposite
so briefly
but just enough

and then
sliding
slowly at first
then faster
faster

I'd been warned of course
everyone had said
don't fall there
The Sickle
sharp icy
a bite carved out
from the snowy ridge
steep
care must be taken
and then
a single breath later
my mind
strangely calm
my body fighting

I thought of the good man
I was leaving
falling out of love
after all this time
I shouldn't have been there
with this partner
with another man
I shouldn't have been there
in that place
all sharpness
and biting wind
but I couldn't see
what a good man
he was

all this
and now
here I was
my axe glancing
again and again
the pick failing to bite
the smooth cold of
a glassy mirror
thousands of years
this ice had been here
I was sliding
faster
down
down
ever downwards
hurtling
the impossibility of it all
don't fall here

and I had
only a single breath ago

I imagine floating
over the abyss
off the edge of the ice
over the headwall
drifting in warm alpine air
jamming with ravens
landing noiselessly
thousands of feet below
on the boulder flats
at the toe of
the Victoria Glacier
that place
where tourists watch
séracs plummet
as they crash onto
Rockies quartzite
ancient ice
dashing into
a million pieces
joining ghosts

the night before
under infinite stars
we had seen a ghost
dressed in rags
worn flannel and wool
rancid breath
the old man had appeared
out of the darkness
and he sat

all night until dawn
under the oily yellow
of the lantern
in that old stone hut
drinking tea
eating pastries
'*Lefroy*' he rasped
his goal for the following day
but in the morning
not a trace of him
and no one recalled
seeing him
but us

and now this
the impossibility of it all
sliding hopelessly
my adze ripping my cheek
on my way
on my journey
dancing with ghosts
and then

I stopped.

the man
I was falling for
this new love
had made the only choice
had done what
all climbers dread
he had thrown himself
over the other side

we fell together
until the rope
held us both
in opposite worlds
on opposite faces
of that icy bite
we hung
each from the same thread

I listened
to the sound
of my breath
against
the pale blue ice
and then
my axe
finally biting
I climbed up
into the sun
into the arms
of the man
to whom I owe
my life

and now
both men have fallen away
another life
all this
so long ago
and yet

Climber

HAZEL BARNARD

CAMILLA BARNARD

There are two reasons why *Climber* is a particularly important image for me. The first is that it depicts the dawning of a new era in my life, and the second is the story of how the drawing came about.

Two months previously I had moved to Sheffield for my dream job, having decided to face the fear of starting out alone in a city I didn't know at the other end of the country, thereby also distancing myself from friends and family. A keen climber and outdoor lover, it was a revelation suddenly to be so close to the Peak District, working in outdoor-adventure publishing.

We parked up along the road from The Fox House pub and climbed the well-worn stile into the field and over the moor – the guys knew their way having been time and time again, Burbage being an accessible area of the Peak with a great selection of classic climbing routes. I was buzzing with anticipation and excitement on the walk-in, taking a nervous wee stop or two. One minute I was making up songs about going bouldering to the tune of *Summer Holiday* – endearing, one hopes? – and the next I was playing it cool, like it was no biggie. Inside though it all seemed a bit surreal to me: *This is on my doorstep; I am going to be able to come here whenever I please.* This place was so beautiful and had such unique climbing that my friends undertake the tedious five-hour motorway slog from Sussex to be among it; for me, it was now just a ten-minute ride away.

We worked our way down from the exposed ridge of gritstone known as Burbage Edge. We picked through boulders and bracken on one-foot-wide tracks, dodging sheep poo down to the main path through the valley and on to the boulders beside it. Walkers, trail runners and mountain bikers passed us as we changed our shoes, immersed in their own adventures. Looking back up towards the edge I could see the tiny shapes of other climbers bobbing about with their brightly coloured pads on their backs, and when the breeze was in the right direction I caught the faint tinkling of nuts, cams and quickdraws. Despite the valley being full of people it felt wild, and the landscape felt vast in comparison to my local haunts in Sussex, the South Downs. Being in the bottom of the valley emphasised this, the edge and two peaks of Higgar Tor and Carl Wark rose around us; I felt dwarfed, but also that I would settle in to this environment most easily.

It was overcast with a hint that the sun may show itself a bit later. We began to warm up on Pock Block, a boulder used for target practice in the Second World War and therefore with 'artificial' holds, but for me, my first ever pull on gritstone. It was like sand caught in resin under my fingertips. Despite these hand-sized pockets the rumours were true: I was going to need some technique to climb on this stuff. In my overexcitement I lapped these warm-up routes as quickly as I could, bouncing from one to the next, and my forearms were burning. Even the easiest problems on that boulder kept their secrets from me; I didn't understand the rock yet. But adrenaline carried me through, as it did for most of the day.

A few boulders later we hiked back up to the edge, as my friends had a route in mind: *David Traverse*. This particular problem was way beyond anything I could hope to complete that day, but I was excited to try it nonetheless. By this point in the day it was exhaustingly hot, and having just ascended the steep slope with pads on our backs, it was a bit of a sweat-fest. I stripped off down to my base layers in an attempt to regain some composure, and discovered that underneath my regular clothes I was dressed like a ninja. I hadn't known how cold it might be – or, as it turned out, how utterly, mind-achingly hot it would be – out on exposed terrain, so in my nervous excitement I had catered for every clothing scenario, apart from, it would seem, tropical heat. I was dressed from head to toe in black merino, and had nothing left I could reasonably remove.

As any climber will tell you, these are not ideal conditions for climbing, and certainly not on gritstone. *David Traverse* involves tiny, hot and sweaty crimps above a steeply sloping, rocky landing. I was diving in at the deep end and not just metaphorically; on one attempt my clammy paws pinged off of the teensy ledges with such sudden velocity that I plunged head first beyond our mats and down the slope, drawing to a halt with my nose just centimetres away from a large rock. *Not* an easy one to style out.

The chosen route and the incessant sun heightened the challenge, but we were also accompanied by a plethora of millipedes on the rock, whom we could only assume were sunbathing. The additional challenge of preserving these tiny lives as they hung out on our hand and footholds was simultaneously amusing and exasperating; the holds may have been clear as we began the route but three or four moves in, the smug critters would have nonchalantly settled back on to the only spots available to cling to.

The rest of the day passed with a summer holidays vibe. We ran into the shade of nearby boulders between climbs. We made that irritating yet oddly satisfying noise produced when blowing through a blade of grass between thumbs. We ate lunch sheltering under trees on tufts of moss and looking out over the valley. Late afternoon, exhausted and with a long journey ahead for my friends, we reluctantly left beautiful Burbage to rehydrate and tend our hot pink skin.

Inevitably, photos of this day were posted on social media and I still grin when I stumble across them now. I have mixed feelings about the book of faces, but on this occasion its resources provided a beautiful opportunity; this is where the story of *Climber* begins.

My mother is a botanical watercolourist – a quietly outstanding one actually, but then I would say that. Sadly this same year she was waiting on two cataract operations, and hadn't been able to see well enough to paint to her fine and detailed standards for several months. In order to release the creative juices she had been hunting for alternative media to play with that didn't require such hawk-eyed vision, and she decided to experiment with dotwork illustration, working from a photo she had found on Facebook of me on *David Traverse*.

Out of the blue I received a photo of the drawing, sent from my dad's phone. I knew the original photo well; I recognised myself immediately. The photo caught me tentatively trying to make my way around the arête near the start of the route, looking down to decide how best to place my feet and shift my weight around ninety degrees.

Despite the poor quality of the photo, I sat stunned for a minute. I was used to being impressed by Mum's work, but I had not seen this media or subject matter from her before, and I knew how poor her sight had become. A new, fledgling talent had been discovered through her unfortunate circumstances, and opportunities opened up for experimentation and development. Furthermore, by pure chance she had chosen to draw from a photo that had captured an emotion-filled moment from a very precious day for me. As I looked closely at her drawing – my right hand placement with middle finger slightly bent, foliage beyond and my inappropriate thermal ninja outfit – it hit home a little more that this was the start of my new life in Sheffield.

Since my inauguration I have explored tors, crags, heathland and summits. I have tried my hand at trad climbing, seen my first grouse and the first peacock butterfly in years. My sunburn has since faded. But the memory of my first day in the Peak endures, the visual component of which made all the richer and more poignant with the creation of *Climber* – something that cuts across the physical distance I have put between close relationships, connecting old and new.

No-Self

HAZEL FINDLAY

If we are asked to look for ourselves, at *what* can we point our fingers? Of course I will point at my chest with firm conviction. Not at my clothes, but at my body. This is where I point, my nail cutting past my woolly jumper. But if it's my body that is me, am I still me when I die and my body returns to the earth? Am I still 'me' when my friend waves my ashes in a ziplock bag? When I look back at photos of myself as a little fat baby, is this me? Throughout my twenty-eight years, cells have one by one fallen from my skin back to earth: flakes of skin, a toenail, clumps of hair.

The earth has a trail of debris following it, a tail of dust. Scientists say that distant planets are easier to locate by these tails than by their bodies; their bodies may be vast and dense but they are difficult to see under the glare of neighbouring stars.

Of course there is something more to being 'me'. There is something it 'feels like' to be me. There is something it feels like to be in *my* head, and this inner me is purer and certainly more permanent than dandruff and fallen hairs.

When I close my eyes I look for this internal me, and all I find are thoughts and feelings, the nature of which are similar to white-capped waves rising and falling in a turbulent ocean. As soon as you track one another fills the gap in its place. I can feel the lump of my body, the mass sucked to earth, and the longer I sit the lighter it feels. There is energy in this lump. The sensations in the felt body are also ever changing. With practice and mental effort, I can enquire into what my left earlobe feels like, and as I watch, 'what it feels like' also changes; an itch builds and then suddenly disappears, a moment later it prickles with the intensity of fire; a second passes and I can't feel it at all. I reach for it fearfully with my fingers to check it hasn't gone. I wonder if this earlobe can give me any clue as to where I might find myself?

After sixth form college thousands of teens travel the world on a gap year looking for themselves. I wonder if any of them may have considered that their 'selves' might be a deep illusion, a best imaginary friend, a trail of debris, not much more than a fallen hair. Can you be both the hunter and the hunted?

I do notice that there are a lot of thoughts spoken with my voice. These thoughts are me. They sound like me and they are saying things I've heard a thousand times before. It's this self I wish I wasn't. The endless record player of a thought-filled self. With effort I can turn down the volume but to switch it off I need help.

Time spent deep in an activity, deep in the woods, deep in exposure, deep on the surface of an ocean, deeply in love – in these wild places with wildness in the heart the self is absent. The absence is not felt or observed because then of course it isn't an absence any more. At first light in the mountains you can bathe in silence without noticing you hear no sounds. Some silences are loud; others are just there.

When I do something completely, my *self* disappears because being and doing doesn't require self. When I exper-ience something grander than I, self disappears. In the shadow of wild lands and vast waters even my tiresome thoughts give up the fight and disappear, leaving my consciousness free to experience without thought or judgement.

Lost in play, lost in effort towards some empty goal, even in fear or doubt, even in discomfort, I drift down not into sleep but into a kind of awakening beyond the waking world; I find my being lost in a maze. In this maze, the self and her little sister the ego cannot follow. Here I can be free from them. And maybe what's left is *me*.

Running with no steps or breaths.

Climbing with no moves.

Watching without thinking.

Sharing without judging.

Dancing without caring.

A day spent without a narrative.

No failure, no success.

Pure absorption.

For some, the concept of no-self is terrifying. Terrifying, as all things which liberate can be.

LIBBY PETER

My firstborn is a millennium baby. She danced inside me as the commotion of a new century burst out into the dark Welsh night. So much so that I wondered if she might choose that auspicious moment to make her entry into the world. But as the revelry tailed off she settled too, staying snug and waiting for a calmer evening.

The point of this detail is that those born close to the turn of a new century are easy to keep track of. You'll never forget their age, and they in turn will help you recall the year of particular adventures. I learnt this recently, as I sat to write '18 Memories' for my daughter's eighteenth birthday.

I learnt too that the unsolicited advice you're handed as a struggling mum about the need to *treasure it, they grow up so quick*, that's totally incomprehensible at the time, turns out to be true. As my millennium baby's birthday approached, a curious panic grew. I wasn't ready. I needed to linger longer in those precious days. So I buried myself deep in the folds of those memories, wrapping them tightly around me. Staying snug.

Many were the outdoor adventures we have shared, seeing familiar landscapes through fresh young eyes and being mesmerised anew. These, I realised, were the moments of clarity within the fuzziness of family, the calm amidst the hurly-burly. Life affirming. Rich. Deeply textured memories indelibly etched, and framed by a mother's skewed, self-indulgent perspective. And love.

Imperfect though it may be, here is number ten.

This was a stolen day. One plucked cheekily from the normal humdrum schedule. A frosty mid-March forecast too good to miss coupled with a lingering hint of winter conditions were occupying my mind. I could see this perfect day looming. They don't come along too often, so they need to be seized. Or so went my logic.

You were thirteen and in Year 8. It was a school day, but you didn't take much persuading. We dropped your too-young-to-join-in sister at school in Llanberis, and we kept driving, up the pass towards Yr Wyddfa. School uniform swapped for thermal and fleece. Crampons and axe instead of schoolbooks weighting your pack. Two truants with smiles of excitement made wide by naughtiness.

Conditions were more alpine than winter, ideal for your first snow and ice climb. Your soft young feet had finally grown enough to fill my spare boots, well, nearly. But stiff winter footwear is unforgiving and cumbersome, especially for the uninitiated, so we strapped boots to packs, and skipped up the Pyg in trainers. Another rule flouted. Breezing nimbly past the clompers, giggling to ourselves and stealing conspiratorial glances.

After an hour or so we scooted off-piste, heading for a round patch of snow that sat squat and resilient in the basin below Wyddfa's so-called Trinity Face – Clogwyn y Garnedd its sing-song birth name. The very first crunch enough to tell us we'd got it right. Here we changed outfits, laced boots and strapped crampons while gazing upwards. Upwards towards a narrow white ribbon of névé and ice that unfurled the length of the broad dark cliff. Shady and hard-frozen. Windless. And empty.

Quiet save for the stamp of crampon spikes biting firm snow, the tinkle of tiny ice shards displaced by tentative pick swings and the rhythmic suck of breath from an exertion unlike any other: full-bodied, calf-screaming, grown-up effort. With a mother's prerogative I fretted and fussed.

About the pace. About the line. Were you too hot, too cold, too tired? Was it too much, too tame?

But all you did was smile, and smile more. And marvel. Like all of us have done on our first acquaintance with a winter wonderland. At the ethereal beauty of the ephemeral. A glimpse of otherworldly perfection within a monochrome landscape. A kind of parallel reality that exists after all in your own backyard.

Your eyes blazed with life, with an excitement I recognised – and envied. And through you once again I felt myself, many years since first knowing. Each rope length took us deeper into the understanding of a beautiful mystery, towards the moment when the impossible becomes possible and a million doors are opened in your mind.

We emerged out of the shadow into bright sun. Blinking. Readjusting. That curious turmoil of being glad it's over, but not wanting it to end. Reluctant to return to normal so soon.

You slumped on the tourist path and soaked up the admiration that inevitably flooded your way from impressed but bemused walkers. Who every one of them on passing us veered rather closer to the edge to peer down to from where we'd appeared. Looking from you to me, and back to you. At our rope, our tangle of gear, our broad, satisfied smiles. Wondering why we were bedecked for winter climbing on such a seemingly benign spring day.

But *Central Trinity* is deep and dark; its secrets well hidden. I'd gambled on it being a rich vein of treasure that March day, and so we found it. Ours to inhabit for a few privileged hours. A pair of sleek ravens our only company. An alternative education of immeasurable value. Mine, as much as yours.

By the Way

SARAH OUTEN

Up over Kinder Scout under
star-splashed skies,
I tiptoe on the gritstone backs of long-gone giants.
Below, traffic homewards bound
and towns glow warmsome.
I am looking for my dad.
(Orion knows)
Night still but for the bog squelch and rock scratch of my boots,
the rush and hurry of Kinder Downfall bursting from the quiet.
Planes weave the sky in a mesh of connect.
A startled bird coughs away in a flap from its nest rest place.
Skirting puddles I try to keep my boots dry
and find ice to crack and crunch, swearing when I skid.
Twirling breath sculpts the stiff air ahead of me momentarily,
condensing into a silver dewy sheen on my hood.

I sleep high and dream of nothingness,
sandwiched between earth and sky.
The next day I eat my lunch on a fog-folded Bleaklow Hill,
pack by my side.
Wandering on, poles tapping,
just as yours once did.
(I found my dad, by the way)
Crossing the bronze-gold blanket of hard-earthed moor
and memory, I feel the enormousness of these twelve years
and the closeness of now.

I chat as we climb Soldier's Lump and you plod steadily
behind.

Remember when you called me a carthorse?
I reckon I'm a chip off the old block, then.
(Our poles in time now.)

The path tracks downward, clinging slope side
and mist creeps up the valley, shrouding us softly.
I remember how, aged ten, the same thing happened on Cadair Idris,
somewhere above the cwm.
You said the top wasn't worth the risk that day
And I agreed. My first retreat.
We stuffed sandwiches and slurped steaming squash huddled behind a rock for shelter,
our packs besides us.

There's a bleakness to my missing you sometimes,
but out here on the hill, you are near.
Even so, I don't want to turn around now, in case I see that you are gone.
So I carry on chatting, poles tapping.

HEATHER DAWE

'There is no substance but light'

    – NAN SHEPHERD, 'EMBODIMENT', *IN THE CAIRNGORMS*

The midday heat was stifling but we found some shade on the trail from the sweet-smelling pine trees as we descended down to Courmayeur. Light came through the canopy, dappled, the cover a welcome respite from the glare of the sun. We were on our second day of running the route of the Tour du Mont Blanc. It was also the second time I had run around this classic long-distance Alpine route. The first time was in July 2010, when I was training for the Ultra-Trail du Mont Blanc, a race I was due to run later that season.

Racing or training for racing used to be my main reasons for spending time in the mountains. I didn't have time to slow down and appreciate just being in the hills; I needed to get to wherever I was going as fast as I could. However, this time, I wasn't there to train for anything. Don't get me wrong, I did try hard, but I intended to savour every moment on the trail.

These days I don't get to spend as much time in the hills as I used to. With two young children waiting for me back home and a high-responsibility job, my free time is squeezed into smaller and smaller spaces. While I still do the odd race, racing itself seems to matter less. In running around the TMB I was getting an intense hit of mountains. These places of natural grandeur have a seemingly unending pull to me. Coming to them helps me to recoil from the everyday; the important things in life become clearer, along with an awareness of who and what I am. This time was precious. I wanted to make it last, and to notice everything that I missed last time.

OPPOSITE – *Aiguille du Midi*
by Heather Dawe

This was my second visit to Courmayeur. Much like the first time I would only be passing through, which I thought was a shame; Courmayeur felt like the kind of place I could stay for a long time. Given its position at the foot of the Italian side of Mont Blanc, Courmayeur has a place in the history of Alpine mountaineering, skiing and all other kinds of mountain-going to rival Chamonix, its French counterpart on the other side of the mountain.

The route of the TMB passes through the narrow alleyways of the village of Dolonne before you cross the river and reach the centre of Courmayeur itself. It was refreshing to walk along streets shaded from the sun – the shadows cast by rows of terraced houses. Deep pink geraniums contrasted with the dark browns and creams of the buildings, the blue of the sky and the greens, browns, greys and dazzling white of the mountains and their tops. This part of the town felt like it had not changed for a hundred years or more. There was a palpable sense of history that got me thinking about the buildings' past residents: who were they, and what adventures had they had in their local mountains?

From Courmayeur we would climb again, out of the Aosta valley, back up into the hills surrounding the massif. The route climbs steeply up to the Bertone hut, from here continuing along the Mont de la Saxe to the summit of the Tête de la Tronche. After this we would descend into the Val Ferret, passing the Bonatti hut to finish our day at the Elena hut and the foot of the Grand Col Ferret, the Italian-Swiss border.

I had been really looking forward to this section of the route; I enjoyed it so much the last time. One of the reasons the TMB is a classic route is because of the wonderful scenery and this, the Italian part of the trail, I had thought the most picturesque, with stunning views of Mont Blanc and its surrounding peaks. While space was limited in my rucksack for this trip, I had allowed myself the luxury of a book, and like the first time I ran the TMB, it was Walter Bonatti's *The Mountains of My Life*. Perhaps this shows I am a creature of habit but it is so thought-provoking – something I keep coming back to. I wanted to feel the same inspiration I had felt the last time: to travel his paths, look up to his mountains, read his words and marvel at the combination of them all.

The Mountains of My Life is Bonatti's account of his development and achievements as a mountaineer, from his time as a boy walking in the foothills of the Alps in northern Italy, to becoming one of the foremost climbers of all time. It is inspiring to read of all of his achievements, but also to read of *how* he achieved them: with his own sense of ethics and values that would have made things harder, but also more honest and pure in his eyes.

Travelling along the paths he traversed, looking up to the massif and the tenacious lines he climbed first – and often solo – filled me with awe. His was a fearsome drive – tremendous courage, a real vision for a great line and a sense of the aesthetic. Given that at the time these were some of the hardest routes ever climbed, his achievements stand out all the more.

Bonatti climbed his last major climb, a solo ascent of the North Face of the Matterhorn, in 1965, when he was thirty-five. After that he still spent much of his time in the mountains, but his focus shifted to travelling around them, capturing them in photography and writing. There is a theme of wilderness and journeying to this work. He still clearly needed to suffer in wild and remote places, but he now indulged his deep appreciation of the spirit of the places he travelled to and through.

I think reading his story helped me to open my mind up to the idea that I could paint mountains as well as run and cycle up them. When I think about it now there had been the hint of a little voice in the back of my head for years, encouraging me to lose some of my inhibitions, forget about the training and racing a little, and to express myself in different ways.

Bonatti's words and spending some more time in 'his' mountains helped me to listen to that voice, to get hold of an easel, canvases and paints, to shake away at least some of my reserve and begin to paint. I honestly think that this is one of the best things I have ever done, and not really because my paintings are any good. The interpretation of art is a subjective thing, the process of creativity all-encompassing, absorbing and relaxing. I can lose myself painting just as much as I can running up a mountainside.

I immerse myself in the creative process in my painting, writing and in the mathematical problem-solving and innovation that forms much of my day job. These three activities are very different from one another but in doing each of them I get my head to the same place. It is an exciting and stimulating place and, paradoxically, a place that calms and even soothes me. When I feel stressed, a little painting, writing or – dare I say it – maths can do me the power of good. Much like going for a run or a bike ride.

More than just the psychological benefits, painting mountains has helped me to see them in a different way, almost with a more enhanced sight. I also now understand what it means when people say there is 'good light'. Late afternoons in November, when the sun casts long shadows on rich autumn colours. Early mornings after rain in March, a pink sky to the east and the promise of a bright spring day. Just two examples of how a scene is made by the state of the light. When I am out running or cycling and notice such a scene, I can't help but comment on this to my companions. They are used to me as a racer in the mountains, focused on exceeding limits and pushing hard, so I don't know what they make of this at times.

When I spend time out in the mountains now I always carry my camera, even when I am racing. I learnt a lesson in August 2014, while running the Sedbergh Hills fell race in the Howgills. These hills are some of my favourite to run in, they lend themselves so well to it: wonderful smooth ridges so well defined and interlinked, and which always feel remote and quiet.

I was having a bad race; my legs felt heavy, and I generally had no zip in me. Just a few miles into the route, contouring the fell side north towards the waterfall Black Force, I resolved to just chill out and enjoy the time in the hills, running along at a pace I could maintain to the finish without blowing. A late summer day out on the fells of Westmorland, there was sunshine and cloud with a breeze that kept you cool while running. Perfect conditions; it doesn't get much better.

One scene in particular from this race stays in my mind. Climbing eastwards out of the valley formed by Langdale Beck, I looked up. The clouds and sun combined to create the dappled light typical of the Yorkshire Dales in summer. This light brought out wonderful colours on the fell side: golden greens, yellows and browns, along with shadows that defined the ripples and lines of the valley with a great deal of depth. I remember feeling so appreciative of this scene, and had a strong desire to paint it, in an attempt to save the colours and the shape of the sky and the fell for my own posterity. I had no camera with me and so could not capture it to paint. I felt frustrated that I had missed this chance, even going back the following weekend to try and get a photograph. The weather was different and so was the light; I will never see that valley in that way again.

Mountains never look the same way twice. The weather, the season and the time of day combine to make them unique at every glance. Sometimes these combinations can be obviously jaw-droppingly beautiful; other times I find

I need to take my time, to look a little longer. The beauty appears as I take the time to properly see, and the associated thrill is an all-consuming experience.

I don't think it's necessary for me to photograph and attempt to paint all the inspiring scenes I see, but sometimes the anticipation of what I could try to capture when painting a mountain scene is at least as thrilling for me as the time I spend in the mountains themselves.

It took us four days to run around the TMB. I loved all of that time, special days in the mountains with memories that will endure. For months after, I painted pictures of the journey and that process transported me back there. Instead of sitting in my home in Yorkshire, I was running along an Alpine trail, breathing the air, seeing the mountains in the summer light.

When I Lived in a Small

ALYSON HALLETT

When I lived in a small cottage on a farm
I was so lonely I talked to insects and sheep.

I watched gulls comb a cloud-spiralled sky
by the slurry-pit,

stared at a robin
who came into the house
and sat on a shelf for thirty minutes.

I loved that loneliness.
The wild daffodils were paler than butter.

One day I set out along the lanes
just as the sun was nibbling trees.
I greeted Morning Man and Loping Dog
then stood in the middle of the road
and turned into a sunflower.

Back then it was easy to become other things.
I was so full of nothing my molecules could rearrange.

Tarmac was no impediment.
Sap came up through my feet,
each green leaf filleted the wind.

Ken the Cross-Dresser
TAMI KNIGHT

Long before Mount Everest became the sought-after, bucket-list item of the over-moneyed wannabes, before grim accidents on the mountain became fodder for bestselling books, before tons of waste were abandoned at the South Col, before climbers had to step over bodies during their quest for summit glory, before all of that there was Ken. But, even before Ken, there was some other bike-owning, three-limbed guy who preferred Coco Chanel to down and fleece and who also dreamed of summit glory. Oh, the horror, the horror.

Ken was contemplating his success as the First one legged cross dresser riding a bicycle to CONKER EV'REST without oxygen .... WHEN ...... TO HIS HORROR .....

Oh

PAULA FLACH

The Lofoten Islands. An archipelago north of the polar circle, carving into the Atlantic like a lithic claw. Although Norway is my second home, the Lofoten Islands had eluded me. In the five years I lived and studied in Bergen, I never made it up to the north of the north.

But for three weeks in a summer not too long ago, in this otherworldly landscape of airy peaks sticking into the wild sky like shrapnel, magnificent beaches and the rolling hills of weather moving in and out, it was going to be just me.

There's always the process of breaking myself in: the pack, the back, the feet, the legs, most of all the head. To exhaust myself physically in the first couple of days has proven a handy technique to make my head and its frantic grind give in. All the thinking in the world will not put one foot in front of the other. As I make my way up the first slopes towards Hermannsdalstinden (1,029 metres), I'm sweating off thoughts, stale feelings, incessant rants about bygone eras and errors, watching them boil down to an unintelligible mumble. They all pale in the straightforwardness of walking, breathing, hydrating and taking a wee in the bushes.

The sensation of fighting and being happily beaten. Every time. Every day. Ever happy. I have always loved the numb yet bubbly feeling when I creep into my sleeping bag after a long day. It's the blissful exhaustion I remember from childhood. Reluctantly going to bed with a day's worth of running, climbing, fighting with my brothers, pulsing in my heavy limbs as I fall asleep. A sensation like sunburn all over and under my skin. After a while the days become a funny blend of light and less light (read: Norwegian summer nights). A blur of walking time, dinner time and bed time.

It was after ten long days of awe-inspiring peaks and meteorological spectacle on a late afternoon, when I set up my tent on a beach in torrential rain. I threw myself into the tent, kicked off my boots and pulled off my socks with my toes. After a little nap I woke up to the sound of more rain drumming on my tent. I could barely be arsed to pull off my long johns to change my underwear. But when I did, something odd happened. I looked down towards my legs and found myself in a state of genuine surprise:

'Oh, I am a female.'

My surprise was so immanent, so strong – I just had to laugh. I laughed and laughed because this was such a bizarre notion.

Oh.

Oh yeah, right. Of course.

I know that this is something I was in the habit of knowing.

The feeling of remembering something I had forgotten all together.

Oh, I am a female.

Here I was, half-naked in a tent, caught by surprise upon realising my own gender at the tender age of twenty-nine. But what surprised me even more was that here, in the middle of nowhere, with nothing on my mind but the blister on my left foot, the weather and what was for dinner, *this* was utterly useless information. For the past weeks, I had been two legs, two arms, a lung and a heart. And that had been enough. I had been a breathing something, wanting to get from here to there and little else.

This peculiar moment in the north of the north is something I treasure. I laugh when I think of it and yet I know that it offered such a profound realisation. What if our gender is not what it's cracked up to be? What if it is just another circumstance we pay far too much attention to, attribute far too much relevance to?

Recently, maybe after turning thirty – who knows, I have become more susceptible to other people's concepts about how men are, how women are, how we are, how they are. *We, they* – all wrapped in a fabric of prejudice woven by insecurities, assumptions and the oh-so-human longing for affirmation and love.

Something that had felt free became laden with expectations from other people, statements cloaked in a brand of cynicism that flies the flag of matter-of-factness. And it scared me. It scared me because these concepts about gender rendered something impartial and open in me, naïve.

Of course our gender is something we can embrace and celebrate. It can be something that lets us relate to one another but it can also be something that draws a line where no line needs to be drawn. Embrace your womanhood, embrace your manhood, but do entertain the notion that there is a living breathing thing beyond that, and that is who we really are.

Besides so many other rewards, the outdoors offers a space to get a taste of that living breathing thing. The lakes we go skinny-dipping in, the mountains we ascend, the heather we nap in and the sand underneath our feet don't care about our gender. I for one didn't realise how much freedom and peace this indifference offers, if we are able to listen.

I limp in the midday lull
to empty beds where church bells
sing me to sleep.

He translates an email
in a flea-ridden albergue:
a reply to Carlos.

Four of us align,
walking from Villafranca
then two fall behind.

He slashes his arms:
seven times for seven sins,
seven caminos.

Village of cobbles
where exhausted pilgrims stretch
on a sea of bunks.

Snapshots from the Camino de Santiago
CATH DRAKE

WATER

In white mountain mist
a dog with a limp barks: *stop*.
Farmer laughs: *friendly*.

Chickens, goats, cows, dogs
in the muddy street. We try
the local cured meat.

Just one for mass
and prayers in English.
His hug smells of ash.

I leave Claudia laughing
with queso, chorizo, book.
No walking today!

Alone on a hill:
deep green valleys, low stone walls,
trickling stream, I sit.

At sunset, I doze
on a warm hay bale, waiting
to see if he'll come.

Snapshots from the Camino de Santiago
CATH DRAKE

Snow

BERNADETTE MCDONALD

He is ahead of me, chugging up the hill with dogged determination. Left. Right. Plant one pole and then the other. Weight the centre of the ski. Push down. Small steps. Don't ease up on your arm pressure. I marvel at my dad, already in his eighties, climbing from 1,660 metres all the way to the summit at 1,900 metres. Where does that lung capacity come from? He smoked for thirty years.

I remember the first few times that we went cross-country skiing. I had somehow convinced him to take up the sport in his seventies. After a lifetime of hard physical labour – on the farm, in the mines, in the war – he agreed to try something completely new. I was excited. Finally, after so many years of learning from my dad – how to drive, to swear, even ride a horse – this was my chance to try and teach him something. I could introduce him to a world of endless shades of white, of wind in your face, and of effortless gliding over fields of frozen feathers. The first few times weren't like that at all. They were more about trying to remain upright and learning about balance and conquering the fear of uncontrolled sliding on two long, flimsy strips of fibreglass. But Dad persisted, and he picked it up pretty quickly. We began exploring the Sovereign Lake hills up on the Okanagan plateau, which are stitched with a labyrinth of ski trails groomed to velvet corduroy perfection each night, primed for the eager morning pilgrims.

We were usually first. Dad never outgrew his habit of rising early. When we arrived at the Sovereign Lake parking lot, he would hustle about with some impatience.

'I'll get the skis out. You run in and get your pass,' he would order. As a season pass holder, he had no need to go inside the modest building that served as a lodge.

'Okay, Dad, but there's no rush.'

'We'd better get going. Before it gets crowded.'

There were three cars in the parking lot, including ours.

When Dad had improved his skills and increased his stamina, we began exploring the longer trails, the steeper trails and, finally, the summit trail.

Up and up we climb, the spruce forest draped in downy white comforters, the tops dipping slightly from the weight. The wan early morning light feels cocoon-like, protecting us from the cold, from the wind. I watch his red jacket advancing up the trail as he skis, his head down, focused on his movements and his breathing. I wonder what he is thinking. Is he savouring the beauty of this place, noticing the elegant lines of the forest, the sublime softness of the snow? Or is he thinking about lunch? I know he can't hear the rhythmic swish of his skis or the soft thud of each pole placement, for he is nearly deaf. I think that is part of the attraction for him. Here, on this trail, this climb, where no one bothers him with questions and stories and offers of assistance, he can, once again, become that independent, completely self-sufficient being, propelling himself to the top of a mountain. He loves going up as much as down.

The higher we climb, the deeper the snow. The forest gradually shifts to alpine fir. Slim as reeds, they appear smaller and smaller as less of their height emerges from the rising snowpack. The rime and the wind create fantastical shapes, and the snow ghosts lean and droop, bowing under the weight as if in a royal receiving line. The morning brightness dims as we inch upward into a squall. The flakes swirl around us, seething past our goggles. We move through the forest of snow ghosts, each of us alone in the privacy of the snowstorm.

We reach the summit and stop for a moment. 'How are

you doing, Dad?' I ask, once I can stand directly in front of him.

He leans on his poles, a little out of breath. 'Yes, I'm good,' he assures me, unzipping his jacket a little to let the steam escape. Despite my fussing, I can see that he is quite pleased with himself. And I'm pretty sure he knows how proud I am of his effort. 'The snow is good this morning,' he says with some authority. 'It's lucky we got up here early.' Of course. We always do. And he's right. The snow is always better in the morning.

Snow is such an inadequate word. The Inuit have dozens of words for it. *Qanik* for falling snow. *Qanittaq* for freshly fallen snow. *Aputi* for snow on the ground. *Pukak* for crystalline snow. *Maujaq* means the kind of snow into which one sinks – soft snow. They even have a word to describe snow mixed with a lead dog's shit: *quinyaya*. This morning at the top of the mountain, we are lucky to have only *qanittaq*, and a bit of *qanik* in the air.

'Don't go crazy on the way down, okay, Dad?' I urge. He has a tendency to ski too fast on the downhills.

'No, I won't. I'll be fine. You go first.'

I refuse, knowing full well that I need to follow him down these hills to make sure he has help in the case of a fall. Off he goes, double-poling, accelerating steadily as the slope steepens. Oh, Dad, slow down. Please, I silently beg. He does nothing to slow himself down. No snowplough. Still double-poling. Straight down in his little crouched position, stiff legs slightly bent, head forward, skis trapped in the track. Has he forgotten that there is a sharp curve coming up? He'll never make it at this velocity.

I ski up beside him, gesticulating with my arms for him to get out of the track, out into the central part of the trail where he can snowplough and regain some control over his speed. He can't hear me, and he isn't looking at me, so intense is his concentration. He enters the curve. It tightens.

He tries to lift one ski out of the track at the last minute, but he miscalculates, crosses his tips and crashes in a heap. Oh my God, Mom will kill me if Dad is hurt. I rush up to him. 'Dad, are you okay? Here, let me help you up.' His fur-trimmed hat is in the snow, his goggles are askew, he has snow in his mouth, and one pole is lodged in a soft snowbank – a *qengaruk*, they would say up north. But miraculously, his limbs are intact. We unclip his skis, retrieve the strewn items, brush them off and reattach everything to the correct body parts. He grins his lopsided grin. I realise he hasn't learned a single lesson from this fall. I grin back. What fun.

Dad had a few special places that he loved to revisit on his ski outings. After coming down off the peak on the Lars Taylor trail, he usually preferred to take the long way back to the lodge via the Silver Queen trail. Undulating like roller waves after a storm, the trail swoops and dips in gentle swells – a relief for the legs after the steep descent from the summit. At the lowest point in the trail, Dad always stopped for a break. He would twist his little fanny pack around, unzip it and reach in for the treat he was carrying. Birdseed. He would open the jar, sprinkle a few seeds on his massive hand, oversized from decades of working on the farm, and lift it up. Grey jays would come winging in, squawking and flapping as they bullied each other for the best stance and the greatest number of seeds. I don't know why this meant so much to Dad, but it was a ritual for him. He would chuckle and chat with the jays, scolding the bullies, urging on the shy ones. The feeding frenzy over, it was time for the long climb back to the lodge and the car, which was always parked in the same position, the special disabled parking spot outside the door of the lodge. I often wondered how Dad had scored the disabled permit, since he clearly wasn't qualified.

As the years sped by, I could see that he was slowing down. It took longer to reach the summit, and he was starting to snowplough on the downhill run, to my great relief. Occasionally, Dad would even suggest a 'green' trail, something he had refused to do in his heyday – his early eighties. His stance was becoming stiffer, his knees more swollen with arthritis, his lungs a little less resilient. But he loved the alpine trails and he refused to give them up: getting out of the valley bottom, being up high, taking in the view, working his body and flying through space. He made all the decisions – which trail to ski on any given day, what time to start, what wax to use and when to go home for lunch. Skiing gave him health and fitness, rosy cheeks and a smile on his face. And he never shied away from a fall.

***

Our Father, who art in heaven,
Hallowed be thy name.

My husband takes off his pack and sets it gently in the snow. My brothers and I watch. He unclasps the top flap, opens the main body of the pack and reaches in. He lifts out a cardboard box wrapped in plastic. It is heavier than it looks.

Thy kingdom come,
Thy will be done,
On earth as it is in heaven.

'Are you guys ready?' he asks.

I watch my brother behind my sunglasses as he reads a poem. We recite the Lord's Prayer. He opens the box, takes a small laundry detergent scoop and scatters some ashes.

Charcoal grey on white. Heavier than the snow, the particles sink, creating countless tiny divots in the perfectly smooth carpet.

Next it is my turn. My brother holds the box and I scatter several scoops of the ashes. Goodbye, Dad. I know you loved this place, where you and the birds met up on your weekly visit. Where you gathered your breath before the long climb back to the car. Whoosh. To the left. Whoosh. To the right. So many ashes.

We take turns, my brothers, my husband and I, returning Dad to the forest, to this little meadow hidden away from the ski trail, yet so near. It's what he asked of us. I have a small avalanche shovel in my pack, and for some reason I feel the need to cover the evidence with some *qanittaq* freshly fallen during the night. Am I tidying up? I'm not sure. Dad always appreciated tidiness.

The ritual done, we retrace our steps out from the meadow, away from Dad's tree and back on to the groomed trail. We glide off together but each alone. I remember what it was like to ski with Dad, always in silence. It was so pleasant to simply ski, with no need for talk. That's the way it is on this day too. I wonder if this ceremony will bring 'closure', as everyone says it will. Maybe, eventually. It doesn't feel like it, though. I still feel completely detached from my emotions, as if they have a life of their own and could erupt at any moment.

It begins to snow. Oh, how beautiful are these feather-light flakes, this *qanik*. The perfectly sculpted track becomes soft around the edges. The falling snow muffles every sound. It seems more silent than usual. I can't even hear my skis. I try to wipe the images of Dad in the last days of his life from my mind. I try to replace them with memories from the trail: the long gliding descents, the purposeful climbs. It's too soon.

I remember hearing about an Inuit tradition where they walk off their anger in the tundra. They walk and walk until it disappears, and then return, their heavy load lightened. Maybe, if I just continue skiing, the rhythm and the sliding and the snow and the silence will ease this pain. I'll keep skiing until they do.

[untitled 2]
KRYSTLE WRIGHT

This image has always remained one of my all-time favourite images. I was camping on Sam Ford Fjord on Baffin Island for a month, documenting twenty-three BASE jumpers from around the world. In the first two weeks of the expedition we experienced incredible weather, however, that wonderful spell ended and we dealt with multiple blizzards in the second half of the trip. During this one particular blizzard, we were huddled inside our base tent and suddenly one team member spotted a local Inuit riding his sled into our camp for a visit. The simplicity of the image has always struck a strong chord with me and even though it appears to be a simple image to capture, I find it's the simplest images that can be the toughest to take. Through the process of developing my eye, I am attracted to complicated situations and hope to solve the situation through creating an image that carries this feel of simplicity.

Through the Snow (Winter 2010)

JUDITH BROWN

Snow creates its own wilderness. It obliterates paths, blurs contours, buries walls. Streams flow through newly made canyons, white depths turning the water a silvered black like the back of old-fashioned mirrors. Footsteps are filled in, or elevated into small ice-structures, carved by wind and changing temperature. Cornices canopy the crag tops, inviting the unwary to walk on air.

Snow fills in the margins between the controlled and the free. It turns landscape into wilderness. 'lawless as snowflakes' wrote Walt Whitman, with a poet's deep perception.

I had forgotten the power of snow. Mild winters had relegated the axe and crampons to the attic. In recent years, encounters with the white stuff had been limited to ski holidays abroad, where crowds of people, clanking lifts, avalanche cannons and overpriced cafes had stripped snow of its mystery. Once, skiing early on a Sierra morning, I saw a coyote slinking from some restaurant bins. Sometimes the wild came in from the cold to feed on the things that civilisation discarded. But he was quickly gone, smelling humans on the wind.

This year it started snowing before Christmas and did not stop. From my windows, I saw a world transformed. I live in the Lake District. Our mountains are small, but with the snow upon them, glittering against a hard blue sky, they were Alps, calling me out via the attic and icy roads, to enter a new world.

I headed for Helvellyn, knowing the road would be treated. The car park at Swirl Crags was empty, the entrance barred by thick ice. Forced further along, I abandoned the car in a side road, and started my walk through the forest. It is mixed woodland here and autumn-browned beech leaves fringed with frost lifted the gloom of the snow-laden conifers. Twigs and branches littered the track, broken beneath the weight of their burden.

I joined the main trail upwards from Wythburn Church, following the footsteps of others along the edge of the forest, overtaking one couple as the path emerged from the trees on to the open fell side. We smiled at each other and agreed it was a grand day.

Deep, uncompacted snow made the steep approach up the side of the hill hard work. I overtook a man struggling with skis on his rucksack. He'd have his reward later, I ventured, skimming down slopes as smooth as silk.

Finally I caught up with another woman, alone except for a terrier so small he ran lightly over the soft surface without breaking through. We exchanged pleasantries about the day, the wonder of sun and snow, sharing an unspoken complicity in the joy of solitude.

I ploughed upwards – on my own now – breaking trail, sometimes the snow crust taking my weight with no more than an indent of my boot sole, sometimes crashing through above the knee. It was hot work in the full sun and still air.

Sweating, I pulled on to the summit ridge. In the distance, figures moved strangely. They were only skiing, but their effortless gliding swoops over the mountain's flanks added to the otherworldliness.

Of course, there were people on the summit; I was on Helvellyn, a 'Wainwright tick'. But there were not many and they were quieter than the summer crowds, as if the deep silence of the snow had fallen on them, too, and stilled the chatter of their minds.

White hills spread all around me, billowing like a giant's bed linen shaken out to air beneath the sun. Ridges I had never seen before, picked out by snow and the blue shadows of the winter sun, curved up the slopes of High Raise, Bowfell, Gable and Scafell to the west; to the north, Skiddaw and Blencathra; with the arms of Catstye Cam and Striding Edge reaching out to High Street in the east and beyond that to the Pennines – clear and sharp in the clarity of Arctic light. The sun struck glitter from frozen tarns, and distant Coniston, long and slim and curved, was a silvered warrior-shield of water, leading the eye to the sea where soon the sun would end its brief passage of a winter's day.

The presence of people on the top and a cold breeze discouraged lingering. A quick drink from my flask, a bite of Christmas cake and I was on my way, heading south along the ridge to the pikes of Nethermost and Dollywaggon Pike. I kept to the edge, or as near as I dared. The cornices formed weird shapes: scooped, cracked and chiselled so that they resembled water-worn limestone. Some blocks were supported by slender necks curving out over the void. Elsewhere, the cornices had snapped off, the fracture line exposing layers of unbonded snow. I was glad I could not hear climbers below; I did not want the serenity of this day smashed by avalanches and a mountain-rescue call.

Following the edge of the mountain, I was out of sight of the main path. The snowpack shone. The only prints except for mine were a fox's. I imagined her trotting across the plateau in the dawn, scavenging the detritus of walkers, but getting short commons compared to the ski-bum coyote. Winter is hard on wildlife. Winters, full winters of snow and ice, are hard on life in general. Even bathed in sunshine, this is not our world. It only takes a small drop in temperature, an increase in the wind, the fading light or a misplaced step to turn beauty into savage hostility.

I know I was not far from a car and a gritted road that would lead me home to a house and a meal and a hot bath. But for several moments standing on that mountain, in a silent world of snow and sky, I felt a stillness as though time itself had stopped, its relentless motion caught in a moment and frozen, just as the deep cold held the movement of water in the icy tarns, of drifting snow in the cornices, and of the wind itself in the breeze-angled frost which fringed the fence wires.

As the sun sank, the rose-gold light seeping across the snow was balanced by long shadows, blue and cold. Where they touched, the warmth was swallowed into silver and gunmetal grey. I was standing on the hinge of the day, the balance point between the plateau and the edge, between travelling through the wilderness as a guest and abandoning myself to full wildness, the winter's night of the mountain.

With a strange emotion that mingled reluctance and relief, I turned downwards, the soft snow allowing a bounding descent of dug-in heels, bringing me quickly to Grisedale Tarn. I took the well-trodden path along the stream: admiring the ice formations; coming slowly back to humanity and civilisation; chatting to walkers up from Manchester, glad for a day of open spaces and far-eyed views; sharing the laughter of children tobogganing in the field above the road.

Snow creates its own wilderness, transient and treasured. I returned to my hearthside, the heritage of 10,000 years of civilisation. But I went back having touched the diamonds that glitter in the frost, feeding that relict spirit in me, 'lawless as snowflakes'.

Ski Tracks

TAMI KNIGHT

Contrasting forms of curvilinear relationships juxtapose aspects of light as reflected on a broad vista of snowscape, speaking to the delineated subgenre of mountain postmodernistic tragedy.

OK, yeah, it's a skier crashed through the ice in a lake and it's supposed to be funny. I found the idea funny enough to both draw it and paint it. Sometimes I laugh at my own jokes. Pathetic, but true.

JEN BENSON

There is a winding brook that falls from the high ground
on the eastern edge of Dartmoor into the green depths of a
wooded cleft. Rising at Seven Lords' Lands near Hemsworthy
Gate, it rushes down past the moss-bright boulders of
Houndtor Valley to its confluence with the Bovey below.

The brook is clear and peat-dark, like fine black tea.
Now still and deep, collecting in round, brown pools; now
flowing fast and foaming, skimming over granite-grey rocks
and spinning wide, white veils as it falls. The heat of a dry
summer thins it to a trickle; heavy rain fills and swells and
excites it, sending it thundering down the hillside, following
the line of its own persistence. One winter, after weeks
of rain, it flowed over the bridges and dammed the roads,
reclaiming the valley as its own.

There are trout in the brook. Their long shadows appear
and disappear, dart and flicker as the sun catches shining
scales in the shallows, then vanish into corners and crevices.
Otters leave their signs scratched into the shingle; bats
bug-hunt at dusk; dippers bob on stream-shined stones.
A pebble, thrown high, falls to the bed with a hollow plunk.
Sticks, dropped off the old clapper bridge, gather speed
and whirl away on an adventure all of their own.

Rain spikes the water's surface: fast, heavy droplets that
bounce and shatter like so many marbles. Beneath a grey sky
the water softens and, silk-like, slides and sheens down its
bouldery chute. Bright sun etches the moorland landscape
into sudden contrasts: blues and greens and yellows and
browns and darkest near black in the shadows. On these
crystal-clear days the brook gleams and sparkles, the sun's
light catching and fragmenting on dimples and ridges

as it swirls and flows, spangling the tops of falls where the smooth, heavy water gathers, ready for its heady plummet.

Slipping out early one morning, the deep green, moss-scented woodland all around, I can hear the brook's gentle crescendo as I approach. Its music is a constant here: a hiss above a rush above a deep thunder; a wild cacophony from which emerges the occasional clear, woody, watery note. This is the sound that lulls me to sleep and greets me each morning here in the valley. An undertone to the birds' chattering and the insects' buzzing and the distant smack of an axe on wood.

I have watched the brook often, at every time of the day and at every time of the year. I've played with it, dangled my toes in it, paddled and splashed in it, welcomed its chill, allowing the sharp fingers of cold to grasp my submerged feet, gasping with a pain that soon subsides to delightful numbness. More than anything else I have simply stood still and watched it, mesmerised by the roll and flow and fall: fast, slow, over, under and around.

Until today it has been a unidirectional brook, bent upon its journey, uninterrupted, downstream. Today, though, I entered it and turned upstream. Barefoot, naked to the thighs, turning the tide I walked against the current, counterflow. I became immersed, not just in the water, but in the brook's own world, absorbing every detail as each busy molecule rushed past. At times great knots of rhododendron and hogweed hedged me in, trapping me on my watery path, forcing me to step on shifting darkness, the unknown beneath my feet. Pushing on, paring the water before me, I felt the stones under my toes in countless shapes, sizes and textures. Some moved underfoot; others remained rock-solid. My skin grazed quartz-sharp granite and slid on the slime of river-rounded rocks. Balancing fear and excitement I stepped, hands flung out, ducking beneath branches so low they laid their leaves upon the stream.

The sudden depth of a dark pool caught me by surprise as the cold water inched further up my skin. Another step and the sun's rays slanted, orange dust into the clear brown, casting a warm sepia below. And all the time, all around, played the river's roaring, rhythmic music, gloriously deafening, reducing the world to just this point where body and water met. I walked as far as my feet could bear on the cold, sharp bed of the brook.

Paddled-out, I escaped that watery world, skin tingling in the warmth of the sun, already longing to return. For I'm happiest walking upstream, surging against the current of expectation, forging my way, counterflow.

Ystradfellte Tree Reflections

NICK DAVIES

To illustrate the surface patterns and the substrate that lies
beneath, transparent images are set over hand-cut lino
embossing. The intention is to give the viewer the feeling
of standing at a water's edge, looking in …

Aqueous

MAB JONES

(Inspired by wild swimmer and artist Natasha Brooks)

The human woman peels away the layers.
Jacket. Gender. Jumper. Class. Something
like an onion, slipping loose of skins;
the stitches of each drape, dissolving;
identity itself unfastened, shimmied out of
like a skirt and left at the side of the lake.

Having shed these skins, then, the human
woman dives, into the earth's blue eye,
as numinous as milk. The swaddling dark is
soothing, makes of her an infant; croons her
to a baby; sings her from her cradling bones;
hymns her to an atom. In the un-sun, star-less

dark, she is *herself* no more. Eventually, naked
spark, she rises; regains what was shriven;
identity's cloak enfolding what was freed.
Patella jewelled with salt; beads of fluid at her
neck, she surges back to being. Reborn, the
human woman stands, and learns herself again.

[untitled 3]
KRYSTLE WRIGHT

Photographing in the water is always an exciting endeavour as it's never ever the same twice; there are so many components to the water. For whatever reason on this particular day, Emma Starritt took a recovery swim after competing in an ocean-swim race off the coast of Mana Island in Fiji. It was late in the afternoon and the angle of the sun lit up the salt crystals in the water, creating this beautiful dreamlike scene. As a mentor once taught me: always be prepared for the unexpected. Even though there is an element of luck involved, one has to create that luck by putting oneself there in the first place.

Taking the Plunge

ANNA FLEMING

Sitting by a lake one moonless night something caught my eye. A small dark mass the size of a soap bar appeared on the surface, standing out against the lake's dim sheen. It moved with determined speed, efficiently cutting through the waters with barely any discernable sound or ripples. I scrambled up for a closer look, but the creature disappeared into the darker shadows. There I glimpsed other lumps moving low and purposefully within the water. Instinct told me these liminal beings were frogs.

I like to think I am no stranger to my own amphibiousness: often when I meet a body of water, be it river, lake or sea, I immerse myself. But, unlike those frogs' dignified power through the water, my dips are rather more raucous affairs. The initial few steps and first plunge carry the full force of crossing a threshold. I teeter on the edge between exultancy and horror. With desperate immediacy my skin tightens, breath shortens and heart pounds, and then, generally, my body adjusts and I temporarily achieve amphibian ease. Sometimes the water is too cold for this. Snow meltwater has the force of fire against my skin, and can only be withstood for the shortest of dips. But whether a short icy plunge or a lengthy bathe, each swim brings an exhilarating high that cleanses, refreshes and renews body and soul. It is a rush of vital living.

The diluvial desire is not for everyone. My dad for example cannot swim and prefers to keep his feet warm and dry. This is a shame, not just because these people miss out on the cold-water exhilaration, but each submersion to the frog's-eye view also brings a further venture into unusual places, perspectives and encounters.

I first came to love the illicit thrill of freshwater bathing in a quarry pool. My mum took us there after school, at weekends or on holidays. The pool sits within a basin, and a short scramble down a steep gravelly slope brings you to the water's edge. Entering the pool, you find yourself in the midst of a rich reforming ecosystem. It is not overtly welcoming: every year the pondweed spreads further across the pool, and dragonflies – small electric-blue damselflies and larger striped hawkers – dive-bomb the swimmer. From the murky depths sometimes a boulder or the metalwork of some ancient rusting vehicle would loom, which, combined with the towering cliffs and prehistoric peregrine calls echoing around, could give a sinister feel to the place. But in summer the water had a warm silky feel that caressed the skin. Here I learnt the indulgence of a skinny dip. Unlike my shrieking skinny dips with family and friends as a youngster in the Atlantic – gasping against the cold and giggling at the strange fun – this pool welcomed the body. As I sank in, the water dissolved the awkward ungainliness of my changing adolescent body, and drifting in temporary fluidity I began to be aware of, and even tentatively appreciate, my own physicality.

That post-industrial site taught me some early lessons on the interrelationship between man, nature and ecosystems. Unlike the sheep-stripped hills and moorland, here one saw nature squat and reclaim the land: a process of diversification. The first settlers, silver birch, rosebay willowherb, valerian and brambles marched across the earth, covering spoil tips, ditches and embankments. At the edge of the workings goat willow and hazel also spread, concealing the old limekiln and quarry buildings that gradually disappeared and decomposed more each year. Sadly though, the quarry owners' benign neglect did not extend to every act of repossession, and the place was subject to an ongoing land dispute.

The company deemed swimming an illegal act of
trespass, which they insisted upon through increasingly
numerous signage. Further signs and life buoys warned that
we humans were in mortal danger near the 'deep water'.
In fairness, someone had died swimming there. He was an
older man whose heart had failed at the shock of the cold
water. This tragedy however did not restrain his daughter's
love of the water. A legendary clash took place when she
returned to the pool the next week. A passer-by spotted
her, and called down, 'You shouldn't swim here; don't you
know someone died here last week?' Our friend's terse roar:
'Yeah! That was my dad!' put a swift end to that discussion.
Generally though, resistance was quieter than this dispute.
In my mind it is typified by the local women who disregarded
each new deterrent in order to share the joy of swimming
with their children and friends. Ultimately, these years of
dispute, trespass and stolen pleasure came abruptly to an
end when the quarry owners finally found an effective
preventative: a two-metre barbed-metal fence encircling
the entire pool. The pondweed now covers the surface,
and we have lost a beautiful spot.

Curiously, the next step in my swimming journey centred
on Liverpool – a city that is not renowned for its clean open-
water swimming spots. While I have friends who have
swum in the docks and park lakes, for some reason that
water never appealed to me; my key discovery during those
tumultuous university years was Britain's mountains.
The half-crazed water babies of my university
mountaineering club introduced me to the unexpected
potential of wilder water. One damp, misty, miserable
October day stands out when, rather than face the inevitable
chilling drenching on the mountains, we traipsed through
the forestry above Betws-y-Coed. At Llyn Elsi, Adam
(a group member with a fearsome reputation for swimming

in unfavourable conditions) stripped off before all our incredulity for a staunch swim. His performance did not end in the water, however. He met the challenge of drying himself with a remarkable solution. In the absence of a towel he did not sacrifice his clothing: he tucked a rolled-up pair of socks inside his wet boxer shorts, donned boots and rucksack, and marched back to the village below. Our laughter, which had dried off by the time we reached the A5, renewed itself whenever we saw the vivid play of emotions rush across the face of every passing carload.

After years of such adventures (weekend and holiday trips to Britain's high places, fiercely soaking up every moment before the exhausted journey home) this year I moved to the Lake District. Living and working in the place has dramatically changed my relationship with it, as I see the sacred adventure playground become imbued with the grainy texture of everyday life. My nearest lake, Grasmere, does not always feel like the 'wildest' place: a busy road spans one edge, broad footpaths lie on the other, you can hire boats or take in the scenery on a bike; the lake is often buzzing with people. Grasmere is also plagued by a peculiar and contradictory modern approach to cleanliness. Around the lake many neatly tied plastic parcels lie at the base of trees, along paths and dangle from branches, swaying in the breeze. Each installation contains the rounded weight of dog faeces, diligently scooped, packaged and placed by their owner. Strangely, when obscured in opaque plastic the faeces become all the more visible. I fantasise about a court case against one of the offending dog owners: a ferocious debate on the relative merits of decomposition and sterilisation. Perhaps they will summon the spirit of ancient Egyptian embalmers to testify to the sacred practice, whereas I will call a compost expert; they then announce an authority on dog dirt parasites, and I find a leading environmentalist to launch forth on the damage of plastic to animals, water systems, ecosystems, the planet, my own sanity … and the case collapses with the over-sufficiency of evidence and banal meaninglessness of it all.

The water however can be a threshold to the wild. I escape there sometimes on a lunch hour: stepping into the water, work and tourists remain at the shore and I delight in the rippling, glimmering mass around me. Of course, the lake does not always glimmer invitingly. I find it much harder to steel myself to action in the rain – the wet weather makes me sink into my waterproof clothing like a snail into its shell. I try to retreat from the irksome elements as far as possible, resenting and thereby intensifying my muffled, dampened, shrunken existence. The moisture always creeps in. On one such morning – Midsummer's Day – when I had been rudely awakened with complaints about my heavy breathing, I stomped down to the lake to try and shake off my rage. There I met the Grasmere skinny dipper. He was taking the waters, despite the time, despite the weather. As he left he called a cheery greeting, and I realised that far from defying the elements, he was taking a real pleasure in it all. In a fit of inspiration, I followed his lead and stripped off. The water was cool, but refreshing, and suddenly the rain transformed from bane to blessing: as it fell upon the surface of the lake it sang. My sullen rage gave way to joy and I returned home to hot tea and apologies.

Loughrigg Tarn is another of my favourite places to swim. In spring, it is one of the few places where the cuckoo still calls. At that time of year, however, a swim is a very cold, loud and short-lived experience. But in the summer months the waters warm up. They do not have the putrid ducky quality of Grasmere and Rydal Water, and with the encircling water lilies, oak trees and glimpses of the Langdale Pikes, it is a taste of paradise. When I took a friend for her first

swim there, she was so enraptured by the experience that
she greeted me the morning after with wide-eyed delight:
'I'm still buzzing from the dip!'

Yet swimming is not always such a successful experience.
On a trip to Eskdale, my partner and I found a series of deep,
enticing pools where the river gorged its way through rock.
Unfortunately, our visit fell on one of those rare May days
that feel like November. The overcast sky loomed overhead,
darkening with the threat of rain, and a bitter wind swept
down the valley from Scafell. Nonetheless, determined not
to be defeated by mere 'conditions', we stripped to the waist
and attempted the first steps towards a swim. Ignoring
the reality suggested by the fact we hadn't yet removed
our upper layers (tops, jumpers, coats and hats were still
firmly in place) we shrieked, shivered, gazed into the cold
depths and then agreed: this was not the day for a swim.
We retreated, gratefully redressed, and walked homewards,
discussing how great it might have been earlier in the day,
or later in the year, and if only the wind hadn't been so cold.
We will return.

A swim I will not repeat took place in Grisedale Tarn.
It lies higher within the mountains, overlooked by three fells
(Fairfield, Dollywaggon Pike and Seat Sandal), and is steeped
in mystical associations. At one end is 'Brothers' Parting
Stone', marking the last place that William Wordsworth
and his brother John saw each other before John was
shipwrecked and drowned in 1805. It is also said that within
the depths of the lake lies the crown of King Dunmail (the
last king of Cumbria) – cast there after his defeat in battle
nearby in AD 945. Oblivious to these associations, on a
warm September afternoon I charged down from Fairfield's
summit, intent on a swim. I was feeling all of the elation that
comes from a day on the fells, and yes, this would be perfect,
the exhilarating climax to a great day. But Grisedale speaks a

different language. As I got closer to the water's edge, it suddenly grew. What had appeared a small, benign body of water from above was suddenly a vast, quiet expanse. As I waded out, I could see each stone lining the bottom with remarkable clarity. Unlike the peaty hues and murky depths of other local lakes, Grisedale's waters are crystal clear. I pushed out and swam, bracing against the cold and waiting for my body to adjust. Ten metres from the shore, I trod water and looked down. I could see my feet below with a rare, perfect clarity – and then in shock – I saw only black below.

Here was the most peculiar awareness of depth: I had a sudden, terrifying sense of an unfathomable void below. It was as if the world had been turned upside down, and the space, the air, the possibilities that usually exist above my head opened below my feet. With the sky still above me, I was suspended in a bizarre midway point – like soloing without a rock face – I was floating in infinite space. I made a beeline for the shore, craving the terra firma of sunshine and descent. It struck me then that the Icelandic belief in the possibility of elf and faery existence was perhaps not so far-fetched in places like this, where my usual composed grasp of space and depth was utterly defeated. Afterwards, a quick internet search confirmed my suspicions: Grisedale is one of the deepest lakes in the Grasmere area. But this understanding has done little to erode the power of that sudden shock of instinctive knowledge.

These escapades with their thrill, fun and freedom are not merely escapism, a way to 'get away from it all'. That stale definition overlooks the essential activeness required to swim in lakes, rivers and the sea. To swim is to act, to shake off the passive role of deskilled spectator that we are relegated to in so many aspects of our lives, now that we do not need to walk to work, grow our own food, or even repair our own possessions. When swimming, we enter an unpredictable arena and use resource, initiative and skill to navigate the difficulties; this renewed agency demands new strands of thought and physicality, fostering further meaningful relationships with the self and with our rich, varied planet.

Waterfall Series No.5

NICK DAVIES

Inspired by my walks in the Glynneath valley where the waterfalls are situated, I have spent many years developing paintings that reflect the movement of water. The surfaces are very textured, using oil, wax and sand to create a semi-sculptural feel.

Diabaig

JEN RANDALL

I took *Diabaig* during the eight months my husband and I
lived in a corner of the Scottish Highlands. We had left our
home of seven years in Glasgow and had one friend up there.
The three of us took to swimming outside: snorkelling in
the rain and fog, exploring canyons on the way up Munros,
wading in rivers as it snowed. This was our favourite spot –
the jetty at Diabaig. Our time living up there will always be
special; we knew it was fleeting and that the space, simplicity
and freedom was something we might never have again.

Thirsty

TAMI KNIGHT

Two pairs of eyeglasses are among the pens, mouse, small box, yellow cedar burl on which the monitor stands, dust rag, hair elastics, gift cards, compact discs, ace bandage, empty tea cup, and Post-it notes in the back office. They're both mine. There's a pair for me to see close up – reading, writing, extracting slivers. The second pair is for distance. Those make visible the birds in my backyard, the potholes when out cycling and the mountains across the inlet. I think about the days when the world was clear to me without looking through glass.

Hiking downhill at an ever-increasing pace, a raging thirst obliterated the memory of our excellent climb, my climbing partner, the thrum of forest life and the late summer soft breeze through the trees. I was so in want of something liquid that had I been handed a jerrycan of gasoline, I'd have gulped it down.

That summer long ago, my pal Jacquie and I had been tearing it up, climbing as much as we could between whacky schedules of work. We scored a couple of matching days off and bingo! We were off to the north-west face of Mount Slesse; the big fang of the North Cascades.

Friends told us water could be had from a small snow patch remaining on the mountain's high shoulder. Contemplating the vertical-mile approach slog we opted for no stove, no tent, don't-need-it-don't-take-it, figuring we'd melt snow with our body heat overnight.

We awoke in the morning in dew-soaked sleeping bags with cold feet; the Nalgene bottle still mostly ice with a grimy slime of water laced with lichen and dead bugs.

But the day was fabulous and we were stoked so nary
a glancing thought was tossed towards the eventual thirst-
riddled epic descent.

I obsessively play solitaire on my computer now that I'm
unemployed. The clutter on my desk is bathed in white
cat fur fluffs delicately wafting. I shuffle to the kitchen and
aimlessly open the fridge door to stare at the contents.
Life has slowed to the pace of a Russian novel and if I
bothered to witness myself, I'd find the same complexities
of anger, despair and sweeping landscapes. But I don't.

I quit my job after being treated to that particular
unpleasantness coming from young colleagues in a
leaderless environment. The inmates were running the
asylum; I jumped from the airplane. I mix my metaphors,
meditate, start things without finishing. After considering
a walk I figure that's exercise enough and return to the
card games. I've evolved into a moss-covered sloth.

'This looks fabulous; I'd like to lead,' said Jacquie at the base
of a sun-splashed corner some distance up the north-west
face of Slesse. We had yet to put the rope on and now the
route steepened so we stopped to belay. We were fit, the day
warm, the rock excellent. 'On belay?' 'Yup, got you!' and up
she scampered like a chipmunk. The route revealed itself
easily; the rock on Slesse varies from dreamy to poo. All we
did was find the dreamy and avoid the poo.

'Off!' drifted down from a long distance above; the rope
went snug and up I went. At her belay we laughed in the
warmth and brilliance of a day on the rock but didn't tarry;
straining the water through our teeth we considered how far
we had to go on how little water we had. I trended up and
left, found a ridge crest and, dammit, we were actually on the
summit fin. The climb was over too soon! We took a pause

on top under the bright blue sky, chattered about previous summits and adventures, knew we were only halfway through this present one, and started our descent.

'You'll never believe what he said about you … he said you're a terrible teacher,' my student said to me, pointing a finger at my colleague. 'I told the director,' she added, 'and she said she'd speak to you.' I'd heard nothing. That night I wrote my letter of resignation. Now at home, the cat loves playing with the laser; we play it frequently.

Heading down the trail now, there was only thirst – dry-tongued and violent. I felt my skin drawing up, howling, cracking, peeling; nothing mattered but that creek so very far below. At an ever-increasing pace we pounded down the trail: down, down, down, to water, water, water. And found it. Clear and sweet in the burbling pools of a mountain creek. Shucking off packs and boots, Jacquie and I lay in the cold water, drinking deep. I took a big breath and went underwater to give thanks.

I have a new job at a family recreation club. I am a gymnastics coach but what I really do is teach kids not to fall on their heads. One student can bend over backwards and touch her head to the small of her back; a trick she does for anybody who looks. Another shits his pants on my second Saturday. The studio in which I work has a modest climbing wall on the northern side. Fibreglass letters vie with fibreglass shapes: elephants, a worm, a gorilla face and a thing reminding me of a chunk of chocolate.

    'My feet hurt on these things,' says a barefoot child, as another student climbs above him without complaint. 'Of course, they're hard on your feet', I say, 'not all of life is pleasant. But soon you'll be jumping on the trampolines.' …

where something else may hurt, but I keep that thought to myself. 'Keep climbing', I suggest, 'and your feet won't hurt any less but you'll still be climbing.' 'Can I please go to the trampolines now?' 'Sure. Off you go.'

Jacquie and I lingered long in the fresh mountain creek that day. Glorious sweet, cold, pure water. Sunlight sparkled off the surface while ripples distorted the reflections from the rocks beneath. Water, like glass, reflecting and refracting light. I felt the fresh breeze blow from the upper reaches of the mountain down the course of the creek. I heard the song of the forest once more. By the time we left the temperature was dropping, shadows lengthening, the water darkening. We got on our way before the water that had refreshed us would cause us to chill.

Do You Remember Me Turkey Blue?

SANDY BENNETT-HABER

In Australia the beach remembers me. It remembers inviting me into its big crashing blue as soon as I could crawl. Over and over it has tugged at my impatient heartstrings while parental hands applied sun cream to my freckled skin. As I grew old enough to do the sun cream myself, its rolling waves have made me late for many a date – other company has only rarely been worth exchanging for beach time. The South Pacific Ocean knows my form well: I've spotted turtles while scuba-diving in its northerly warmth, surprised it plunging into cold springtime depths near a remote southern lighthouse, gone wetsuited to swim with the dolphins and skinny-dipped on the eve of the new millennium. It probably remembers more than I do, and a little that I would rather forget.

The saltwater of Turkey is a blank slate: I don't know it and it doesn't know me. But two months' travelling in the desert have me beyond pleased to make its acquaintance. Every uncomfortable, sleepless second on the overnight bus from Göreme to Olympos is almost worth it to be within walking distance of the Mediterranean. I arrive at my tree-house hostel early in the morning, dump my backpack, pass through the ancient ruins without a second glance and am looking at the curve of the bay soon after the fumes of the bus have dissipated.

I walk slowly across sharp rocks, already hot at 9.00 a.m., wade through the refreshing cool of the stream that runs into the bay, set my things down on the shaded edge of the rocky beach and at long last take that first plunge to say, 'Hello Turkey blue, it's nice to meet you'.

Getting to know you takes time. In Olympos I see your welcoming public face, you are a calm and easy host. Toddlers, tired travellers and too-toned-tricep bulgers mingle on your shores. The bikinied and the burkinied alike are at home in the calm of your waters. After falling asleep on your shores I wake, plunge, am refreshed, sleep, plunge, repeat … I enjoy your bounty, and float anonymously amongst the crowd. You have to take care of the babies and the flailers. I float calmly, giggle as I somersault backwards and luxuriate as you draw the heat from my skin. I know I am just one amongst many happy bathers here.

You don't know me yet and I know very little of you, but your memory holds layers of stories – that much I remember from my history classes. Perhaps if I'd paid more attention I would know you better now. I try to remedy this by wandering along the shady pathways into your past. In the dark green of the forest, trailing down from the mountains sitting sentry above the bay I shun the well-trodden footpaths, taking those that threaten to peter out to nothing. Relics of the once-great Lycian city crumble on either side of the stream that flows out to the bay. Walking amongst the overgrown ruins of this city by the sea I might be exploring the fantasy castle of Cair Paravel from Narnia. At any moment a great lion and perhaps an umbrella-carrying faun might walk over the crumbling mosaic floor, through the vine-entwined archway and, mistaking me for Lucy, pause to greet me near the lonely pillars … but no, the approaching footsteps belong to some other T-shirt-and-shorts-clad travellers, no more magic than myself.

The spell of Narnia broken, I try to see your reality: stone doorways to nowhere and a pillaged sarcophagus that might have housed the remains of Marcus Aurelius. Once this tumbled city stood tall on your shores and you watched as rich and poor went about their business. Lives happened here, traders bought and sold, lovers laughed and lost, pirates invaded, crusaders stopped over, and finally the city was abandoned to crumble. All this was witnessed by the mountains, the stones in the walls and you.

What am I next to all that? Only another newly arrived and soon to depart girl, tramping about with her camera and lying in the shade with her book in between swims – hardly worthy of notice, and yet I want us to know each other.

I journey on, pestering you by boat now, though I choose to think of it as establishing our friendship. I see glinting bays, remote villages only made accessible by you, busy beaches cluttered with bright umbrellas, quiet rocky coves and more fragments of ancient cities sinking into your depths. You happily boast many picturesque locations and condescend to let us drop anchor awhile. Much as I love the sights, this is what I yearn for. I plunge off the edge of our sailboat, plummeting deep into your cool blue – the oxygen cut off from my lungs until I can kick myself back to the surface.

'Again!' my body sings. 'Again!'

At night, waiting for your calm roll to rock me asleep, I look up from my spot on deck and watch for shooting stars with a smile on my face. I do like getting to know you.

After a few days' swimming, fishing, turtle-spotting and paddling about in your playground we arrive at St Nicholas Island and moor for the night under Byzantine ruins. Many others are moored here already. This is another of your safe harbours, where crew and happy human cargo can float for the night within view of tall masts, flying flags, your sparkle and craggy rocks. My fellow travellers put on their walking shoes and take the tender ashore to explore the island's crumbling stone churches, pathways and, most tantalisingly, the possible burial place of the original Santa Claus. I eschew

dry-land exploring and strip down to my bikini once more.
I want the mermaid's-eye view of the island.

Feeling thoroughly acquainted with you by now my
freestyle strokes are confident: head down for three: exhale,
head up for one: inhale, head down, head up … kicking all
the way. I am quickly greeted by another sheltered cove and
I swim on. Head up for three: inhale and glimpse sun-warmed
ruins, head down for three: exhale and the underwater
silence envelops me. All is blue, head up, and I am looking
ahead, eager to see all that there is to see.

I swim 'just around the next corner' through a few friendly
little bays; your waters are warm and shallow. Looking up
I see a boat mate – a land explorer. Does he glimpse this
strange fish? I wave … no; he is intent on ancient sights.
I swim on, sandy coves beckoning with private beaches
just for me, but sunbathing does not interest me. I forget
about the land and swim, immersing my whole self in
your blue welcome.

Rounding a corner I find myself peering down at the
roots of the island. It plunges into your chill inky depths.
Plunges down and rears up in steep bluffs – no longer
inviting the weary swimmer to clamber ashore. It is exciting,
for a little while. Your waters become choppy. My passage
is no longer easy. My arms are no longer fresh. My freestyle
flounders. Head down for two: exhale. Head up for four:
inhale saltwater. Then I putter out. I switch to sidestroke,
anxious to avoid simply floating on my back. You will send
me backwards, or worse if I stay still. I am tired. I have
become one of the flailers, but you do not take care of me.
I push on. Going back must be further now than going
forward? Besides, I am still eager to see all you have
to show me.

I am greeted with more outward edges, more ink-dark
water. Night is still a distant thing, but the sun has gone

from this side of the island. Tired and eager for a shortcut I abandon my cautious hold to the shoreline and move into your open reaches. I put my head down, determined to go for it. But, no longer hugging the island, I make slow, sloppy progress. My determination means nothing against your steel cut and thrust. I am swallowing your brine unwillingly. Stopping often to gauge my lack of progress. Struggling to get nowhere. I am way out of my depth. My limbs shake. I panic.

Fear churns through me. I am alone and panicked with only you, and you show me your most indifferent face. But I can be stubborn too. As you will not offer any support I must be practical, rely on myself. I get it together, push the panic down and give up my attempt to make it to the distant corner. I swim back to the island and lose my shortcut, but keep my head above your dark, choppy indifference.

The fear is still there as I aim myself at a rocky ledge, and finally, you help. You lift me on a wave and spit me ashore. A sodden limpet, I cling to land, away from your rock and roll – is this where I belong after all? On my rock I lay still, breathing in, out, in, out and there are no lashes of salt choking my lungs. In my humiliated defeat I will not meet your eye. I rise, a mermaid no longer, Ariel transformed on bare salt-sogged feet and shaky legs. I clamber up the rocky edge. At the top of the outcrop there is a discovery awaiting me: I am almost at the tip of the island's nose, the point I have been trying for, where I would have swum back to the sunny side of the island and into your calm waters once more. Do I hear you snicker?

I ignore you, my body is reverberating fatigue and my moment of panic was real. Whatever you may think of me I am not so much disappointed to have nearly made it, as I am pleased that I will make it. I climb down the opposite side and hesitate for a moment, before dropping back into you

– welcome or not. I am not keen to continue my swim, but I trust my tired legs more in the water than on steep rock.

I doggy-paddle slowly towards the boat masts of home accompanied by your quieter self. My water-lust is sated for today, and I am finally confident that you, Turkey blue, will remember this foolish flotsam.

She Collects the Puddles and Lakes She Swims Each Year

PAULA FLACH

This piece is inspired by the wonderful film *My Big White Thighs & Me* by Hannah Maia; a film about swimming in the wild and making peace with your own body. I haven't swum in the wild all that much. I'm good with cold air, but cold water is a different deal. Swimming in wild places is a new challenge for me and I look forward to all the lakes I'll try and swim in the Norwegian summer.

Llanerch Wake

NICK DAVIES

To illustrate the reflected surface patterns of trees situated at this location, transparent images are set over hand-cut lino embossing to give the viewer the illusion of standing at a water's edge, looking in …

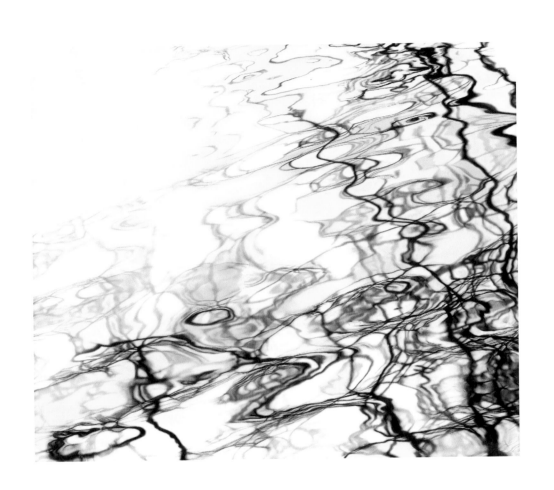

Emergence
CLAIRE GIORDANO

Storm clouds build over the glaciated peak of Mount Baker, and the last of the early summer light silhouettes tall evergreens. It is a moment of transition, as shadows build on the brilliantly white snow and in the gathering clouds. And in that moment, there is a tangible energy; like watching the hairs on the neck of the landscape lift in anticipation and uncertainty.

As the first mountain I summited, I find myself continually drawn to Mount Baker in person and in my paintings. This mountain, like a wise grandfather, taught me how art can be a conduit between people and place. I return to the mountain trails year after year, finding my artist's voice in line and shadow. I paint to share the experience of nature; the incredible joy alongside inherent risk and undercurrent of mystery and loss. In the shadows of jagged ridges and the open space of an expansive sky, I am connected to a greater whole.

It's dark, he's covered
in mud, fell off his bike twice:
long way to see you.

They switch on the lights,
and we eat platters like kings,
toast with wine, take a taxi.

On the road again, he texts:
you are good beautiful,
a nice thing to find.

A quiet albergue
fills with pilgrim sock smell, chat,
clutter, arguments.

She asks all of us:
please can you pray for my son.
Eating flan, we nod.

Snapshots from the Camino de Santiago
CATH DRAKE

On an early start,
I take mint tea in a fog
and Fillepe appears.

I walk and talk, he passes
then waits for me with wine carafe
almost empty, all smiles.

Dopey happiness
with boiled octopus, hierbas,
slinking into sleep.

He's too fast for me
and disappears over a hill,
waves tiny waves.

I walk through sunlit gum trees,
dreaming of my home town
and stories to tell.

We sleep-in, savour
tea and cake before walking
non-stop to Mount Joy.

Snapshots from the Camino de Santiago
CATH DRAKE

Running on the Roof of the World

LILY DYU

A deep rumble echoed around the valley and below me,
the cloudy debris of a small avalanche swept over the grey,
crevasse-crumpled glacier that snaked around the mountain.
Breathing hard, I made slow progress up the zigzag path.
My eyes followed the trail to the snow line, and here the
first runner appeared – the ever-cheery Nepali, Phudorjee.
He was on his way to the finish before I was even a third
of the way up to the turnaround point.

At 4,000 metres the sun was intense, loosening ice
and rock, making the surrounding peaks gleam. Jagged
chains of mountains ran in every direction, while above
a raptor floated on thermals, silhouetted against the blue.
Looking down, glacial lakes were sapphires studding the
pristine steel-grey and white. In the silence, I could hear
my heart pounding in my chest. Manaslu means 'mountain
of the spirit' in Sanskrit, and in this place where heaven
and earth meet, it felt as if the thin air was imbued with
an otherworldly spirit.

If you had told me as a plump, sport-hating teenager
that one day I would run with world-class athletes, I would
have looked up for a flock of pigs. Yet here I was in Nepal,
with forty others in a 'sky race', climbing a vertical kilometre
from Samagaon village to Manaslu Base Camp and back.
This was the fifth of a seven-stage foot race around Manaslu,
the world's eighth highest mountain. A keen runner since
my twenties and addicted to the flow of trail running,
I had entered the race simply to run in a country I had
long wished to see.

With rocky paths, huge climbs and steep, difficult
descents, this was to be the toughest thing I had ever done.

An early wake-up call would stir us from warm sleeping bags to a breakfast of porridge and pancakes. While the crew and mules moved our bags on to the next trekking lodge, I was usually out running and walking for most of the daylight hours, long after the fastest competitors had finished the day's fifteen to twenty-mile stage.

In the lodge at Samagaon we sat round a long wooden table waiting for dinner. We hadn't washed in days – apart from using wet wipes or maybe buying a thermos of hot water – but wrapped in down jackets and hats, the only smell was from the smoky fire that barely warmed the air. Accommodation was basic and generally without heating and electricity, while squat-toilets and frozen water showed us how much we took for granted in our Western lives. Conditions of life here were hard and this was a couple of years before the region was to be stricken by the 2015 earthquake.

Three runners talked in French, sharing some foie gras and crackers they had brought with them. I cradled a mug of tea; it had been bitterly cold since the sun dropped out of the valley at 2.30 p.m. Another group were laughing, playing a word game. Time passed slowly and life-long friendships were cemented as the evening stretched out. Some German trekkers, still wearing head torches, sat at another table, already feasting on vegetable *momos*.

Ignorant of the effects that altitude and exertion could have on my body, I was horrified that day when my period arrived early. After asking around the women runners, we eventually peered into the kitchen to speak with the lodge owner's wife. She insisted on selling me one of her precious packs of sanitary pads; there, at over 3,000 metres and days from the nearest town, I knew they couldn't be easily replaced.

Eventually, that night I went to sleep in a simple, bare

room with no windowpanes, listening all night to the banshee wind wailing outside. I was cocooned, fully dressed, in my sleeping bag against temperatures of -20 °C. At another lodge, where I'd arrived in darkness when most of the others were already eating, I slept amongst sacks of rice and lentils in a tiny room doubling as a storeroom.

Yet the cold and physical hardships were small discomforts in exchange for what we experienced. In deep gorges, to the roar of the glacial river far below, undulating trails led us through Buddhist and Hindu mountain villages floating on jade terraces. Mountainsides were threaded with tumbling waterfalls, whose mists were laced with rainbows. In the high, wild valleys, yaks grazed next to fields of barley, while family harvests of orange-green squashes rested on tin rooftops. Our stomachs lurched as we crossed delicate suspension bridges between forests tinted with autumn colours. The beauty and scale of our surroundings was hard to absorb.

Passing through villages, children shouted, 'Namaste!' as they walked to school, some breaking into a run alongside us. In one hamlet, we passed boys hitting a shuttlecock back and forth, while another pushed along on a broken plank on wheels – a home-made skateboard. Lazy Asian dogs dozed outside doorways, disinterested in the runners, while inside women were often seen sweeping – poor, but house-proud.

Higher up, some villages had no schools, and here young children played in streams, colourfully wrapped against the cold; little padded Buddhas with matted hair and runny noses. Nearby, a scrawny chicken chased a baby goat. On paths smelling of yak and mule dung, a young girl hurried past, glancing at us with shy curiosity. She carried a bundle of firewood she had collected, the conical basket strapped to her forehead.

In these mountains, living felt intensified: a sip of hot

lemon at a checkpoint, the taste of the yak cheese and chapatti unwrapped for lunch, the scent of pine, the breath of chimney smoke, the red of poinsettia growing alongside the path.

One night, we stayed in a Buddhist monastery after a long climb through enchanted forests had brought us to the ancient 'Shangri-La' village at Hinang Gompa. Here, the night sky of a billion stars arching across the purple-blackness between glistening peaks is etched forever in my mind. Looking up, I felt at once both my insignificance and the wonder of my being there.

The next morning, we woke to the sounds of bells and prayer wheels being turned. After breakfast we retreated from the bitter morning and assembled inside the shadowy temple, lit with candles and thick with incense. A small group of crimsoned monks and nuns murmured prayers, some looking as ancient as the trees in the valley below. We were making a donation of solar lights to the village as we had in all the places we stayed – either that or donations to hydroelectric schemes. The head monk blessed each of us, wrapping a cream scarf around our necks before sending us on our way down the valley. We were grateful to finally run and warm up.

Our highest stay was in Samdo, at 3,800 metres on the Tibetan border, where we spent two nights acclimatising to the altitude. Here, a gentle couple invited our group of curious runners to sit around their dung-heated hearth in a dim, two-room dwelling, warmed by yaks kept beneath. While huddled there, our head guide, Dhir, pointed his trekking pole towards a shelf stacked with cookware and ornaments saying, 'That gives the young people dreams, then they don't want to stay here any more'. He was pointing at a small television set, which we were surprised to see amongst the pans.

Meanwhile, outside in a dusty courtyard, a meeting was taking place to decide who would stay to look after the village that winter when the rest of the inhabitants moved lower down the valley to trade yak products and wait for spring. In a nearby field, children played an impromptu game of cricket, immune to the plunging afternoon temperatures.

Some young people do return after their education in the cities. In Samdo, Rajiv, who had been schooled in India through outside sponsorship, came back to teach, also opening an internet cafe and introducing basic computers to the school. Our expedition doctor, Paresh, had been trained in Kathmandu and the UK, but returned to Nepal to work. He said that many of his fellow students stayed abroad after their training, comparing Nepal life with their new lives in the West, which, 'made them want things they didn't need before'.

Before the sky race in Samagaon, we organised a one-mile fun run for the school children in which a shrieking tornado of a hundred dust-streaked maroon uniforms blew through the village. In the prize-giving ceremony, each child was given a picture book brought from Kathmandu on muleback, along with our supplies.

Sat on a wall after watching the children pass, Paresh and I talked about the coming development of the region, including the arrival of roads and whether this would deter trekkers – the main source of income. But many villages had no medical facilities or nursing outposts and he told me a story of when he was on a medical posting in a remote mountain village and was woken in the middle of the night by shouting below his room. A young woman in labour had been carried for twelve hours down the trails from a higher village. Her family and neighbours had been unable to deal with serious complications that had arisen during the birth. 'Would you deny them a road here?' he asked me.

To climb over the 5,160-metre Larkya La pass, the highest point of our journey, we left Samdo at 4 a.m. walking on moonlit paths – a chain of bobbing lights in the coal-black valley – until sunrise daubed the cathedral summits orange-pink. Unseasonal snow and ice made the route treacherous, so the porters lifted boulders into frozen streams to make them easier for us to cross. Below blinding sun, it was a long, slow trek through deep snow occasionally pitted with bird tracks. I was breathless with the altitude and eventually the porter-cook Kumar took my pack to carry it the final mile to the pass. Here, elated and emotional, we rested as prayer flags fluttered against dazzling white and blue and a panorama of iconic peaks.

I have never felt so alive as on that journey down from the pass. Kumar guided me carefully down icy slopes and time stood still as I concentrated on the placing of every single footstep. Resting, we watched our mules struggling on the steep, glistening mountainside as the sun dropped. In deepening dusk we reached the rocky moraine where I kept tripping through tiredness until we finally arrived in darkness amongst the flickering lights of Bimtang. Here, greeted by the other runners, my tears flowed with exhaustion and relief.

On the last race stage, we descended through forests and along riverside trails, feeling the sweet air thicken and the warmth on our skin as we dropped 2,000 metres to the finish at Dharapani. To the music of the rushing river and birdsong, I ran slowly, drinking in views of the valleys hung with cloud, not wanting the journey to end.

A long, bumpy bus ride on monsoon-wrecked roads took us back to Kathmandu. Through open windows blowing in dust and fumes I saw colourful saris in the fields and men building roads by hand. Leaving the mountains was a dislocation; after the sanctuary and space, we were overwhelmed by traffic, noise and the sight of people glued to mobile phones. I wondered how the mountain villages would change as Manaslu becomes developed, and thought about my own village in the Welsh borders where forty years ago many hill farms had no electricity and pumped their water from springs.

Somehow this sport-hating schoolgirl managed a respectable twenty-fifth place in the race. I had gone to Nepal to feed my running habit with the beauty of the mountains but what the experience really showed me was what is essential in my life and what can be stripped away. While every runner trod the same sky-high trails around Manaslu, I was making my very own journey of self-discovery.

RUTH WIGGINS

the girls keep diaries
in which they stick
feathers and five-leaf clovers
and draw stick-girls glugging litres
of peaty brown water
fresh from the hut roof
fresh from the river.
Their ankles are bitten and bush-scraped
their socks stuck with thistles.
And there are ex-gymnasts
with splinted toes and breasts that
never really showed.
And girls sleeping four-abreast
in bunks with boys
that can't believe their luck
but know, tomorrow
they'll be gone.
And there's river-vaulting Coraline
peeing on the track and yelling
at the bush chickens
to leave her arse alone.
And Dorothea Brewster in her liver spots
her gung-ho calves, her name
embroidered on her pack
in case her heart.
And there's Ronit and Hagit
Odin's two green crows
sad and soggy in their military ponchos.
And other girls prepared to make
merino knickers last

another day, or so.
And Sylvia, the ornithologist's daughter
impersonating penguins
in the dark on Rakiura.
And there are Canadians glowing
in mountain lakes
and girls like eels making out in rivers.
And grubby girls wolfing
pumpkin soup for breakfast
trading fruit for salt
and salt for fruit
leaving stuff behind
to allow for ukuleles.
And girls being saved from drowning
by nothing more than
thick tweed capes and their own resources.
And the track is filled with their
gleeful squawking
as they hike on shoestrings
duck clear of rangers
and yum-hum-yum over cups of cocoa
and palms of trail mix.
Suddenly magicking
a couscous and chorizo picnic.
And first-timers with bright pink
baptised feet, sanctified by dye
that leaks from bright red sneakers.
And legs in little shorts and bangles
cross-hatched and crescent-mooned
at the ankle and the hip

old marks of negotiation.
And girls with theodolites
and heavy rifles
staring hard at sucked clean
duck bones.
All of them, out there, in the sun
and wind, making their way
under the tremendous.

She Collects all the Trees She Climbed That Summer

PAULA FLACH

I suppose this is a younger version of myself. Growing up, I climbed all the apple trees in our garden. I can remember what it was like to take a bite from a freshly picked apple, sitting in the canopy, discovering a new perspective, a new hideout and feeling very cool. To see the trees changing through the seasons always reminds me of the fact that nothing is forever and yet trees seem to have something stoic about them. They stay put, no matter the weather and will blossom every spring. That is why they are such a source of comfort to me.

Bouldering
KATHRYN HUMMEL

The simplicity appeals to her.
She prefers bare hands
to ropes and tethers.
The rock face stays so close
she thinks she sees
a reassuring expression
on its brow.

Boulders, like scriptures
once settled their curves
into place. No prophet can
shift them from their pursuits
of happily gathering moss
and withstanding water.

She says she can feel
her way through problems,
tentative fingers wan with chalk.
Boulders are not mountains:
their troubles seldom soar
more than twenty feet.
Gods make their homes
at higher altitudes.
If she does not climb,
she will traverse for a while,
limning a plausible ascent.

(The simplicity appealed to her:
a train towards the mountains.
His face held a tint of chalk;
his eyes, the fathomless blue
of a pitched tent of sky, presented
a most difficult veneer to climb.)

The desired view never reached,
she holds a static sequence,
silently mapping the traverses
of a lesser kindred.
No doubt she considers
this abstraction:
the summit is not the focus
if the walls close near enough.

Falling is the inevitable conclusion.
The carriage of the train
has carried through, just
never towards the mountain.
A boulder only hurts
the way in which it's meant to.

Bouldering at Ardmair Beach
DEZIREE WILSON

I have always been drawn to compositions with unusual perspectives, and in this piece the climber is an abstract, geometric presence immersed within the soft flow of the shapes and patterns around her.

This is a very tactile piece: her hand, rather than her face, is the focal point and I wanted to convey the unique sensation of climbing on Torridonian Sandstone, with its rich textures and mellow hues.

Snails
TAMI KNIGHT

What might have been passing through my brain at the time I drew this: although a probable billion years of evolution separates terrestrial pulmonated gastropod molluscs from the human form reliant on unroped climbing of smaller geologic forms for recreation, the snail possesses sufficient associative reasoning to understand the shell he/she carries about upon his/her dorsal surface exists with more function than that of the boulderer. But it is also true that snails *à la bourguignonne* are delicious.

The Grampians
JEN RANDALL

When I took this shot of Al bouldering in the Australian Grampians I knew I was unwell, but didn't realise my appendix had ruptured and I would spend the next ten days in intensive care. This was the culmination of months of poor health which forced a huge shift in my attitude towards myself — I could no longer take for granted that my body would work no matter what I asked of it, a surprisingly difficult idea to come to terms with. This was my last day of living with my old outlook, and I'm glad I got this image of Al doing his thing that day, playing on the rocks, being my rock.

K'é yił yał tx'i': Saying Something

LESLIE HSU OH

Along the Tohickon, which may originate from a Lenape word meaning 'Deer Bone Creek', cliffs of red Lockatong argillite and Brunswick shale form the unusual High Rocks of Pennsylvania. I balance beneath the shadow of leaves stubborn enough to withstand the blunt of winter, my feet planted on either side of an exposed root, on the slippery slopes of a gorge entangled with fallen trunks. Through my zoom lens, I study my husband, a splash of warmth against a canvas of rock, as he lifts our giggling kids above his head by their belay loops. Apart from the sound of a hawk landing on a branch of tulip poplar, the roar of the creek drowns even the noise of my breath.

My camera rests gently on the wispy black locks of our five-month-old. She is so quiet, so content swinging her legs from the sling across my chest that I sometimes forget she is now part of this scene. On the buttress above, our eleven-year-old, Kyra, has worked her way up a crack and is trying to find a hold on friable shale. Since age three, she has been determined to be the first woman of colour to win a NASCAR race or to earn an Olympic medal in snowboard cross.

I feel my heart quicken when I see the uncertain dance of her fingers across a smooth lip. I don't want those fingers to become mine, scarred at age twenty-one, fingertips raw from scaling peaks after I lost both my birth mother and brother to liver cancer. I don't want her to climb the way I did, without fear, the higher and riskier the better, because I thought the worst thing that could happen to me had already taken place, and I was untouchable.

Kyra sweeps glances of awe at the world from her height.

Only after she touches the roots of a cedar growing at the top of the cliff does she take the time to find me.

Everything in the Diné (Navajo) world view is bound by four sacred mountains. Shortly after my birth mother died, I met Ursula Knoki-Wilson of the Táchii'nii or Red Running into Water People clan. She folded my rough and calloused hands inside hers. I became the daughter she never had.

She used to tell me to call her Rez Mom, but now she has borne the weight of Mom longer than my birth mother did. One day, we walked in Monument Valley until the red sand worked its way into the creases of our faces, hands and heels, between our toes and in our hair. Thunderbird Mesa towered above us. Cooling off in its shade, Mom bent down and sifted the earth through her fingers. When she lifted her hand, the red sand coated my face.

'The thunder gods are housed here. Sometimes I will come here and sit, just to feel the energy. The sand will protect you wherever you go,' Mom said, and then she handed me a bag to collect some of it. Resting my right hand on the earth, I felt heat lick like flames up my arm. I closed my eyes and sank on both knees.

Mom pointed at the Ye'ii rainbow in sand paintings and explained that mountains talk to each other. She taught me how to orient myself according to the four sacred mountains. Placed at the cardinal points to deflect or absorb harmful energies, they allow life on earth to exist in balance.

The East Mountain, Mount Blanca, also known as 'white shell mountain', is in Alamosa, Colorado. Mount Blanca is a fourteener, the highest and most difficult of the four sacred mountains to climb. Symbolising thinking, the east is the direction of new beginnings or a time to revisit a journey.

Riley, our three-year-old, orders her dad around while he fits her into a full-body harness. At the start of the trail to High Rocks, she had already organised us into her favourite characters from *Frozen*: her dad is Kristoff, she is Elsa, I am Anna, and Joe Forte – the learning centre director at the resort where my kids train on a snowboarding competition team – is Olaf.

Our eight-year-old, Ethan, sits at Joe's feet and flips through a trad rack. Ethan runs his tongue nervously over his front teeth held in place by a splint after a freak flag football accident ruined his snowboard season. His forehead crinkles with irritation until suddenly a smile ripples across his face. Later, Ethan tells me that he's finally figured out what to do with his life. He could become 'Batman' through rock climbing.

Joe is spending his day off with us. With years of experience as a guide, he thinks Kyra could develop more trust in herself through the more methodical, slow-paced act of rock climbing. 'There's no one she has to compete against except herself,' he said.

Now, he speaks to Kyra in a steady voice, calming her as she struggles to remove an extra cam he placed in a crack. Beneath a worn beanie and kind hazel eyes, you'd never know that he struggles with Lyme disease. He always places the needs of others before his own, even though he suffers from headaches, blurred vision and dizziness. This is the character of the man roped to my kids: as selfless as the mountains he loves to climb and ride.

The South Mountain, Mount Taylor, also known as 'turquoise mountain', is in Grants, New Mexico. Mount Taylor can be hiked within a day and is the easiest to scale. The south is the direction of planning and learning, a time to implement and act.

A few months before we climbed at High Rocks, Mom came to help me with the birth of our fourth child. In front of our fireplace, she kneaded dough to satisfy my craving for fry bread. Her fingers pulled then pushed the dough against the mixing bowl in a rhythm that always brought me back to the Rez. *Thwump. Thwump.* Like the sound of my weaving fork against the yarn in my loom.

'Everything has a spirit and needs to be respected.' *Thwump. Thwump.* 'In Navajo, we call it *K'é yił yał tx'i'*, which means "it's saying something with a kinship feeling". We are all related. That's why you have to ask permission of the mountain, water, trees before you have an adventure on them.' *Thwump. Thwump.* 'You don't just come into my house without knocking on my door, right?'

Sprawled on her stomach, Kyra wrote down every word she heard. Ethan paused his Minecraft game to listen. 'Mountains all over the globe are our cousins,' Mom said. 'They are mothers and protectors. That's why you have to do the honouring.' *Thwump. Thwump.* 'When I went to Tibet and stood at the foot of Everest, I could feel the rhythm of that mountain in my soul. Before I climbed her, I found a water source.' Mom explained that girls offer white shell or coral while the boys offer turquoise or obsidian. 'If you don't have any of these things, then you can pick a young flower with berries or a rose. Make sure you face east, like the way I taught you to always begin with Mount Blanca, then move in a clockwise direction while saying a prayer.'

I wrote down the prayer that Mom taught us and memorised it. Before we leave the house, I always remember to ask permission from mountains, rivers and trees, but once I'm outdoors, much to my frustration, I forget.

A month before we climbed at High Rocks, I left the baby and toddler with my neighbour and hiked with my husband, Kyra, Ethan, Joe and several other snowboard coaches to a glacial pothole that rose out of the Susquehanna, a Lenape word that means 'Muddy River'. The temperature that day hovered around 25 °F, so cold I could see my breath condense into phantom curls.

We crossed sections of the river in various stages of thaw or freeze. A whisper of movement underneath the ice lured me to an oak leaf preserved at the peak of autumn with all its imperfections. I felt a kinship to remnants of another season. A breeze long gone had carved artful designs deep into a portion of the river that had pooled and frozen, thick and white.

Trailing after the others, I hid behind my camera. When I could no longer hear footsteps, I took off my gloves and ran my hand over the surface of the river, reading the patterns of snow that melted into rain, rain that froze into sheets of sleet.

A wind blew my down jacket open. I looked over my shoulder, feeling exposed, and then pulled the hood down over my eyes. Without the chatter of my kids, I became uncomfortably aware of the thoughts that have hunted me since my birth mother died. Life pools in my cupped hands like water, and I can't figure out how to hold on to moments of joy before they slip through my fingers: a mother's kiss, a first ascent, the words I do, the tiniest baby toes.

At a fork in the trail, my husband waited as still as the river birch grove, pretending to check his email. He shook his head when I tangled my cold gloveless hands in his.

The first time my kids climbed outdoors was two years ago at the New River Gorge. On that day, my son froze on a pitch too scared to move. Kyle Kent, a grade school teacher and rock climbing instructor, counterbalance-rappelled to our son, and he said the only words that could've gotten our stubborn little Batman to take action: 'I'm your Robin.' A half hour later, my son became the first in our family to rappel off the Endless Wall.

When my son, my daughter, then my husband disappeared into a sea of trees without a sound and it was my turn to walk backward down a lip that receded with each step, I choked. I wished that I had rappelled first so I could have captured photos of the first time our kids found courage. My husband never asks why I take so many pictures, and I never say what's running beneath the surface, like decayed and swollen wisps buoying up. I no longer remember what my brother and mother look like or how their arms feel around me. When my mother was dying, I swore to her, *I won't get married. I won't have kids without you.* I thought those words could hurt her enough to hang on to life. She had told me that becoming a mother was the best thing that ever happened to her. I didn't want to understand what that meant without her. I broke that oath, and now I see how it protected me from loss.

Every muscle strained to stay on the micro-edge foothold, refusing to obey Kyle who yelled, 'Let go'.

Our mind is our biggest limiting factor and our own impression of ourselves is what holds us back, Joe once said. By the time my toes slipped, my mind had already moved on to concerns about how my body had changed with childbirth. Gravity yanked me swiftly down into branches and leaves. I entered another dimension, dark yet familiar, layered in sandstone and shale deposited by ancient rivers. And just as every muscle snapped against spinning, I leant back against the ropes and gave into leaves drifting down on my face like snow.

The West Mountain, San Francisco Peaks, also known as 'abalone shell mountain', is in Flagstaff, Arizona. As Arizona's highest summit, San Francisco Peaks is the most visited of the four sacred mountains. Symbolising the activities of daily living, the west is the direction where you learn from your mistakes.

The coaches eyed the rising Susquehanna River nervously as Kyra and Ethan used etriers to aid past the first six feet of blank schist to reach the start holds. Neither of them seemed to mind the cold or the difficulty. Joe's teaching of Arno Ilgner's irrational vs. rational fear was working:

'If you checked your harness, rope, karabiners and your belay device and you communicate with your partner well, you should have no fear of hitting the ground. That's an irrational fear. We know all the systems are in place. It's safe. How would you apply that to snowboarding?'

'Being afraid at a competition to do a trick I've practised all season?'

'Yes, if you've done the trick a million times, you have no reason to be scared. On the flipside, if there's another athlete that's trying to pressure you into doing a trick you've never done before, that's a rational fear.'

As I packed away my camera and made my way towards the family, my daughter asked for another turn. By that time, the river, nearly the same colour as the schist, had risen about a foot. Without informing her belayer, Joe, Kyra leapt on to the first etrier and missed. Because the rope wasn't yet taut, she fell waist deep into water so cold and translucent that you could count the rocks beneath the surface.

Before I could react, Joe pulled Kyra out of the water and back on to the wall. Everyone extended a hand to bring her in, but she shook her head. Only one word did she utter between shivered gasps, 'climb'.

When I arrived at her side, she had completed the pitch twice as fast as she did earlier. The coaches patted her on the back. Kyra handed Joe back the soaked fingerless gloves that he'd lent her. He poured her a cup of hot chocolate and told her about another one of Arno's concepts: 'You have to have a certain amount of confidence and trust in yourself but not so much ego that you think you are undefeatable.' I checked her little hands. Nothing bleeding, just mud caked beneath the nails. I kissed her fingers before I warmed them in my gloves. None of us had brought an extra change of clothes, and she still had about a mile or two to hike out to the car in her wet shoes and socks. She didn't seem to mind.

She announced, punctuating each word with chattering teeth, 'Never give up'.

The North Mountain, Hesperus Peak or 'obsidian mountain', is north of Mancos, Colorado. Hikers say their favourite of the four is Hesperus because of the difficulty of route finding. The north is the direction for reflection and evaluation, for looking forward.

Back at the gorge, the Tohickon rushes by with such force that it's hard for us to hear each other. Joe says to Ethan, 'If the crack in the rock is parallel, then you use a cam. If the crack forms a V, then you need a nut. See how they are shaped like a wedge?' He smooths his red beard.

Balancing one hand against the red argillite, a trad rack in the other, Ethan braces his feet in etriers against the rock. There is no top rope, but he is only about a foot off the ground, and Joe can look over his shoulder to evaluate his placements. I wish that someone like Joe had introduced me to climbing in this way instead of college boys showing off their skills to try to win my heart.

When he and Joe finally settle upon the nut that fits the crack best, Ethan shifts his weight to one etrier. Joe helps him unclip the other and reattach it to the protection he just placed.

'OK, now ease on to it. Do you think it will hold you? Give it a good bounce to make sure.' The pieces of gear hanging around Joe's waist clang against each other like bells. It's a sound I fell in love with in college when I joined the mountaineering club at the University of Sussex.

Once Ethan realises the protection he placed is solid, he looks at me and raises his eyebrows in delight. He gingerly aids up and down a few times, then repeats it with more confidence. I can see his mind firing connections: from this 'aha' moment to the triumph he felt the first time he scaled a fifty-five-foot climbing wall to perhaps one day rescuing someone by aiding through nightfall or storms.

Our three-year-old climbed for the first time at a gym last year. Without any hesitation, she moved from one colourful hold to the next with an elegance I had no idea someone so young could possess. There was no expression on her face, as if she had been doing it for years. At High Rocks, the minute her dad hoists her up on the argillite, she bursts into laughter. She can't concentrate. As if the sun, wind, water or rocks are having a conversation with her, she keeps bubbling over with giggles. Joe boulders at her side, patiently returning her hands and feet to holds. She's more interested in 'flying', and the only words she manages to string together over and over are: 'Olaf don't fall down.'

As we pack up to leave, our son takes off his helmet. He is careless with it, and it rolls, then bounces faster and faster down the gorge towards the creek. The descent is so long that we can still hear one *thunk* after another even though it has disappeared from sight. He retrieves it only to let it slip out of his fingers once again. This time, he collapses in a heap of frustration. Joe smiles at me and nods. None of us hike down the gorge to help my daughter and son. We can't hear what they are saying, but after a long while we see my daughter return with the helmet, which she then promptly clips to her bag. My son trails far behind her. Both of them complain that they got more bruises from retrieving the helmet than from the climb.

I am overwhelmed with pride and jealousy that my kids are understanding lessons that have taken my lifetime to earn.

They will be eager to tell their friends what happened,
but disappointed that no one gets it, because how do you
explain something as personal as realising a profound truth
about yourself?

Without acknowledging that there is the weight of
a baby strapped to my chest, I feel my bones settle reluctantly
into my new relationship with climbing. *It's OK*, I comfort
myself. *It's no longer all about you.*

K'é yił yał tx'i' I whisper to my five-month-old. Like
my camera, she zooms in on Joe, her siblings, her dad, the
cliffs, creek, trees. She chews on the cowhide of my climbing
gloves. Her eyes are wide, fascinated by all that is being said.
When I place her hands against the argillite warm from
the sun, she presses her palms gently against the stone the
same way that she touches my face and hands when she
nurses, both hesitant and confident, an exchange so private
and raw I have not acknowledged it until now.

I don't need to tell her to respect the mountain. She already
knows how.

[untitled 4]

KRYSTLE WRIGHT

The subtle moments can be key to what can make or break a photograph. I was working with rock climber Steph Davis in her hometown of Moab, Utah, on a short film. We were shooting away, but as the wind began to pick up I noticed her hair blowing in the wind and the photographer in me overrode the situation; I switched back to taking photos and waited for the right moment where the hair perfectly fanned out behind her. To me, this subtle action gives so much energy and flow to the final photo and represents the strong spirit that Steph carries into her climbing and everyday life.

The Climb
HELEN MORT

The climb begins
under cigarette-smoke sky
below a rock's mossed fin.

No. The climb begins
in sinew, muscles twitching
on the landscape's brim

above a saucer-valley:
Langdale, crossed by rivers
you could almost dive in.

No. The climb begins
with rain, battering
the Old Dungeon Ghyll

where you sit
with your battered guidebook
by the battered windowsill.

The climb begins
in your ice-blue Ford,
the wheels' manic spin,

your face framed
in the rear-view mirror briefly
like a lost twin,

the radio, your rucksack
the pale quartz
of your chin.

The climb begins
with thought, its static
electricity against your skin,

begins with stone-fall
memory, loud,
the way the thunder sings,

a baritone, how lightning
once forked past you
left the branches singed.

The climb begins
with sleepless nights
the strange stone of your whim.

The climb begins
on days there's nothing to be done
and nothing you can bring,

the silence you live in,
holding a quickdraw
bright as a wedding ring.

The climb begins
on a nameless slab, the place
where the holds get thin,

now thinner. It begins
in your held breath
your sudden rictus grin,

your reach, your
balance, how a magpie
skims and settles, prim

below you in the copse,
how the sheep all scatter
with their scattered din,

how a walker passes,
holds his solitude
like a priceless violin,

how the river starts
to beckon you, glassy
with its dark mossed trim.

The climb begins
the moment you undress
and start to swim.

You start the climb
when you squint up at the buttress
for the perfect line,

when you lift your hands
and they fit the rhyolite
like an end-rhyme.

No. You start the climb
with thoughts that knock
against each other, chime

like the gear
on your harness, twist
like a sling's blue twine

when you're so alive
you lift a bottle and your tongue
turns water into wine

when you stand
unmoved
in summer's firing line

and Cumbria's a glass
of heat, the sun's
a slice of lemon rind.

You start the climb
when you're done with patience,
done with being kind.

when your nerve
is a thin seam of frozen
water, stilled in wintertime

no matter how your feet
slip, how the holds
are slick with shine.

You start the climb
with the sudden focus
of a mountain guide,

you start it
like a careful mourner
at a gold-edged shrine

you start it
in the last vertebrae
of your long spine

in your blunt fingernails
and your hair's
loose vine

you start with
breath and blood
that could be mine.

You start the climb
with no love, no name,
no fear in the mind.

Mad Hatter's Gully in Winter

DEZIREE WILSON

Gaudi-like gargoyles emerge out of the ice in this piece, menacing and threatening to overwhelm the intrepid little climber as he inches his way up the route towards safety. I wanted to convey the sense of being at the mercy of the elements in winter, and the fearlessness needed to battle against them.

The psychedelic style evolved quite spontaneously, and added nicely to the dizzying effect.

Unmapping
KATIE IVES

On a winter's dusk, the walls of Maple Canyon, Utah, seem like narrow, gothic corridors, lengthened by shadows. Cobblestones glow golden as they fade. The desert air stills with the long light of a nave. Shimmers of frozen waterfalls pour from the rim, flickering like starlight. All day, my climbing partner and I have wandered this place by ourselves. A recent storm seems to have kept others away. Drifts of new snow part around our feet. Amid the silence and the dim, the shouts of summer sport climbers are unimaginable. At nightfall, my friend turns the corner of an ice flow. Following, I look up, and I think his headlamp shines down at me. But it's only the rising moon. Soon afterward, I join him at the top of the climb, yet that moment of uncertainty stays in my mind – a slip of vision, in which a man might transform, briefly, into an orb of silver light.

For the past nine years, after moving back to New England, I've often waited until sunset before hiking to the base of winter climbs. I prefer to leave the parking lot just as most climbers are returning to their cars, the sounds of their ice screws clinking in the brittle air. Soon the noise of the road becomes muffled. On the trail, the numbers of passers-by dwindle. Twilight flows in along the tracks of animal feet like a silent tide. Even the small wild nooks of Vermont seem to expand – for the span of an evening – into the immensities of space, entire universes of shadows trapped between tree roots.

To be 'benighted' is often thought of as one of the dangers of climbing. Those who return late to town are 'overdue'. At times, I've worried that someone seeing my distant light on a mountainside might think, falsely, that I'm in trouble.

And yet, as all habitual night climbers know, to seek out
darkness deliberately can open unexpected portals into
wonder and awe. New Englanders Guy and Laura Waterman
wrote in their 1993 book, *Wilderness Ethics*:

> '*Anyone who has been out overdue on a walk as darkness*
> *comes in knows that night doesn't fall … It wells up*
> *beneath the dark trees, the thick-branched evergreens*
> *first, and, after milling around for some time in the dense*
> *forest, gradually steals out into the clearings, keeping close*
> *to the ground. Only gradually does it rise and envelop*
> *people and the works of people.*'

I've walked late at night since I was a young girl, when the
full moon lured me from my upstairs bedroom, softly down
the wooden stairs of my mother's Massachusetts house
and out the door – where the quiet streets turned to rivers
of white light and the woods swayed in the wind. Through
dense hemlock branches, rays of moon scattered like charts
of constellations across the forest floor. I imagined, then, that
nightfall could restore something I thought I'd already lost –
a childhood world tinged with magic and waking dreams.

Older, now, I've felt an increasing restlessness drawing
me back to the dark. In a headlamp beam, the world breaks
into luminous fragments. I meander up climbs, collecting
images: a green gully lined with sea-glass ice; a single
star above an invisible ridge. During the day, blurred
memories of evening flow back through my mind like
clouds through trees, catching on branches – an inner
floating realm of nightwoods and wildwoods, of half-lights
and phosphorescent colours.

In Western Europe, historians say, early forms of
modern mountaineering arose alongside the advances
of 'Enlightenment'. Dragons and goblins, once believed

to haunt the heights, 'disappeared before the early dawn of science', or so the Victorian climber Leslie Stephen declared in 1871, in his famous book on alpinism, *The Playground of Europe*. Meanwhile, the introduction of gaslights to streets and factories allowed the growth of surveillance and the increase of production. But there were also those – a few climbers, poets, *flâneurs* and foot travellers – who fled the spreading of both metaphorical and artificial light: alpinists such as Geoffrey Winthrop Young, who wrote of a form of climbing that might remain 'a romance apart, unsocialised', describing scenes of lantern-lit ascents, of glaciers re-enchanted by nightfall and blazing stars. In *Nightwalking* (2015), Matthew Beaumont explains, 'The act of nightwalking … carved out dark spaces in the landscape, cityscape and psyche that promised an escape from the penetrating glare of the Enlightenment.' At a time when imperial explorers and armies sought to subjugate the last 'blanks on the map' – imposing their own boundaries, terms and claims, while obscuring local homelands, names and stories – night voyagers might still have dreamed of practising a movement in reverse: 'to wander is to uncharter.'

Today's communications technologies allow climbers to spotlight even the most isolated and solitary ascents. It's worth recalling what it is we might be losing – as the inheritors of a tradition that distrusts what can't be easily documented and seen. In *The Outermost House*, the naturalist Henry Beston declared, 'for with the banishment of night from the experience of man, there vanishes as well a religious emotion, a poetic mood, which gives depths to the adventures of humanity.' I've long imagined a counter narrative of mountaineering – annals of shadowy figures left out by tales of development and progress; recollections of unknowing and of silence.

Of course, I'm not always alone at night. I've encountered

parties of climbers – overtaken by darkness because of a slow
partner or a stuck rope – staggering home through falling
snow. Occasionally, I've seen the lights of other voluntary
night wanderers, rising like stars up ice gullies towards the
sky. Skiing into Smugglers' Notch one winter, I paused at
a sudden red glow in a cave above me. A group of women
were drinking champagne by firelight. Later, as I clambered
up a staircase of fragile yellow ice, the wind shifted, for an
instant, and their distant voices rose like a flock of birds
winging through the dark.

The climbing writer Peter Haan and I once imagined
a fellowship of 'gloamers' – some hidden gathering of those
who have used climbing for centuries as a way to explore
the twilit spaces, those gloaming thresholds between light
and dark, waking and dreaming, existence and void. Far
from the glare of commercial imagery and the headlines of
mainstreamed stories, the numbers of such quiet adventurers
are vaster than anyone knows. In the 1937 book *The Night
Climbers of Cambridge*, Whipplesnaith (a pseudonym) wrote
of British students who made nocturnal ascents of rooftops
and spires – an un-history of trespassing:

> *'The blanket of dark hides each group of climbers from its
> neighbours, muffles up a thousand deeds of valour, and
> almost entirely prevents the existence of dangerous rivalry
> … Some records doubtless exist, in diaries or in log-books
> kept by individuals and by ephemeral night climbing
> societies. But the written word, where it exists, is kept
> hidden away … '*

From late night and early alpine starts, I've become familiar
with the way that darkness creates new and ever-shifting
otherworlds. After many hours of no sleep, in Wyoming's
Teton Range, I'd see murky figures and strange animals

flow through the shadows of crevices and boulders across my peripheral vision – altitude-induced hallucinations that seemed almost companionable.

In *Alpinist* 20, the climber Peter Croft wrote of his predawn approaches to Sierra climbs: 'I have a proclivity for moonlit adventures, an attraction to my own superstitious fear,' he explained. 'I also want to be ready to witness the sorcery of night, those times, particularly alone, when my imagination flares up at a furtive, nocturnal rustling or an unexpected draft of warm air.' In the dead of night, soft sounds and scarce-lit images can seem to tear the curtain of the world – as if a wayfarer might cast a sudden glance to the other side.

There's a common theme in climbing stories that the thought of death creates a sharpened passion for existence. Alpinists, trapped on high, icy slopes, have felt the return of the sun as an explosion of colour and hope. But perhaps repeated time spent in the shadows brings us something more: a way of habituating ourselves, gradually, with the shortness of all human lives; an acceptance of our inevitable crossing, one day, beyond the edge of sight.

Lines of frost glitter on cliff walls like the contours of old maps. Beyond the rock, cascades of ice have melted and refrozen, forming new landscapes of curtains and caves. In darkness, I enter a frozen chimney, and the world shrinks to the miniature hills and valleys of each foot of ice, luminous in my headlamp beam. When I reach the top, the world beyond the climb returns – all at once – unfamiliar, incomprehensible, recreated. It's as though I have to learn the names and identities of objects again. Descending into the forest, I startle at strange blue bands glowing across snowdrifts: I'd forgotten that the moon cast shadows between the trees.

In *A Field Guide to Getting Lost* (2005), Rebecca Solnit wrote,

'Between words is silence … behind every map's information is what's left out, the unmapped and the unmappable.' I'm not seeking to chart the pathways of my mind. I don't desire to follow the oft-repeated slogans that urge me to discover myself. I wish, instead, like Solnit, to let go of boundaries and definitions. To escape, for a while, a society in which everything appears deceptively – at times oppressively – well lit. To realise that even the known world is fundamentally unknown to me. To dissolve the false outlines of my self in ice, rock, snow and sky.

It's in unmapping that climbers may come closest to finding what we seek. Not in the claiming of a route or in the recording of numbers. Juxtaposed against the nightfall of mortality, all illusions of the value of conquest, measurement and attainment fall away. 'What we gain is a bit like dark matter,' John Porter writes of alpinism in *One Day as a Tiger* (2014). 'We know it has to be there because we know the universe has mass and energy we cannot see or measure, but we cannot say what it is. But the fact is, we keep on trying to describe it.'

One summer in the Tetons, sometime after midnight, a friend and I got lost descending the West Ledges of Mount Owen. A passing hailstorm, a tumble of rocks and a cut rope had slowed our journey up the long, spiny ridge of *Serendipity Arête*, and by the time we'd clambered on to the summit, the sky had turned from rich gold to dusky violet to starlit black. When the moon sank, we were still midway down a steep, cold maze of scree-covered slabs and sudden cliff bands, old rappel slings and narrow terraces. Soon disoriented, we traversed back and forth, scrambling deeper into shadows, unable to glimpse the Valhalla Canyon floor.

With each step downward, the topography only seemed to grow. And when the sun finally rose, most of the West

Ledges still stretched below us like a grey and crumpled page
– as if in all our nocturnal wandering, we'd arrived nowhere
closer to the end. With daylight, we quickly got back on route
and stumbled into the heat of lower altitudes and the dust of
busy hiking trails. Yet it's the evening that I remember most:
the dying flare of moonlight; the sound of water dripping
and stones falling into invisible depths; the weariness of
turning from dead end to dead end until we'd gone far
off route, and the walls seemed to unravel into endless,
branching paths, each one equally wrong and true.

For within the centre of that vertical labyrinth, I've
realised, there was something I'd known in other moments,
walking or climbing or writing all night into the blue glow
of dawn, until my steps, my words or breaths seemed to
fall into some older, forgotten rhythm. That unexpected gift
of extending myself – body, mind and soul – to the edges
of all I know, believing that by sheer exhaustion and by
wonder I might encounter something like grace. For this,
then, is either the temptation or the promise of the wild
and the dark: to be so lost, that one might at last be found.

unshod to meet the flints

POLLY ATKIN

By the weird light of the cloudy moon
I was walking bare-soled on small sharp stones
from our own front yard to the next-door lawn

slowly, palms parallel to the ground
as if to press the flint teeth down.
They hurt, but not enough for sound

to swoop from my mouth as a bat or a moth
through the thick grey night. I didn't cry out.
The air was woven of heavy cloth.

Did I reach the grass? Did I lay on the moss?
Was it wet and cool on my back, on my calves?
Did I sit like a statue on the podium rock

till the clouds dissolved? I had no song
but forward movement. Over sharp stones
inching, unshod, home.

She Always Collects Her Starter Number in Stones Along the Way

PAULA FLACH

I drew this woman and her odd habit because I find runners' discipline and their willingness to struggle, to compete and to push themselves so remarkable. The challenges we set for ourselves (such as collecting your starter number in stones along the way) are such a personal thing. Sometimes we keep them secret, sometimes we tell others to ensure we stick with them. Sometimes, the sweetest victories are those that no one else knows about.

A Pattern-Maker for Memories

ALICE MADDICOTT

Down the narrow lane where hills have fallen to meet fields then sea, I stand, shoes grass-roofed and dampening, and walk on. There is something about just here, traces I can almost touch, invisible lines in the sky, a moment where moving, one place to another, there's an atmosphere change – a flicker-of-light boundary.

By the tabbied shallows that sing, leaves curl like a small child's fingers and fall – weaving the air with flickers. Rocks like friendly monsters wait to cross the river – slowly and surely.

I sometimes wonder about all the movement that we cannot see. The momentum of nature – the subtle drift. I walk – I drift – and the landscape moves around me in flutters of wings and air and seeds. Leaves talk if you listen carefully. My translation is rusty, but there is something in their whispers – stories. I think they know what lies beneath.

I picture it like this: a walnut fell and was broken and inside was a small thing that was gentle and understood the field where it landed and the network of trees that held hands underground – a filigree web of mushrooms and root threads.

The county is held together by these.

They transmit messages.

They see childhood and holidays and love, once and then again later, though different. Sea and lakes and moors – the ponies nibble and words dart on to their tongues. Released in neighs the wind takes them and then birds hear and then clouds fall and then Somerset is drenched by them – in everything, these stories and pictures – sepia soggy in faded sunlight.

The land is divided up in sounds and feelings. These are pulsed out for unsuspecting bystanders to soak in, to take away on day trips to cities and sea.

But there is one place I always come back to, one place where the depth of woods and tumbled streams control the atmosphere around them to a point where it is like they are in a force field of their own creation – a net in which to keep their feelings safe. My mind lifts whenever I walk into it. And even though it is not a part of my county I have ever lived in, I feel memories come back to me – as if the roots have sucked them up just for the occasion and are scattering them out in invisible showers to land like pollen on my nose and get sneezed in.

Even the memories of trips to other countries are held here. The trees can sense across oceans and trigger miniature tsunamis of lost thought.

My eyes itch, almost allergic to the sudden season of them. I blink and look around.

There are not many houses round here and those that are near wear straw hats like farmer witches. Their windows glint like diamond teeth, shutters of violet eyelashes.

I walk to remember. I walk to forget. I walk to think and to not think. I close my eyes and feel the lids redden like rose-tinted blood glasses; I open my eyes and see small things: an abandoned nest, a beetle running home, and old man's beard drifts like sparse snow past the whisked tails of ponies and subtle breeze talk.

There is a wall of ferns leaking my moss memories to the footpath.

Bracken spills a shanty town of beauty for voles and insects up the wooded slopes to the secret dens of red deer and hedgehogs. Goshawks fly like magic arrows missing trunks, and I cannot believe that I live normally and don't see this. How when I get dressed I don't imagine how flowers could be dresses, how bees might wear pollen to impress their friends through the streets of the wild flower city and the skyscrapers of bark for birds and the cracked maps of ant kingdoms.

It is just as much a reality as a street of houses. There is nothing to say it isn't. Just age and a changed way of seeing; as a child I thought slugs had magic kingdoms.

Sun-drenched patterns dance for lost discos.

And always the memories hiding in pockets like bits of forgotten fluff and scrumpled paper.

The river carved the valley like the centre of a cake. Trees are a crumbled topping – sweetened broccoli hair. I crouch by the water and watch the light scatter shadows for minnows and warm the aching pebbles. It is both loud and quiet. A background song and a dialogue of endless, almost lost, conversation.

I often wonder if rivers are like memories. Logically you should never be able to see the same bit of water again, it has flowed past. But I was thinking about this, and it's always there somewhere, this bit of water from a river: out to sea, in the clouds, drunk by thirsty trees, waiting like distant thoughts under a layer of deceptively sunny weather. Each time you look at the same place in a river there's still water there, which looks the same as that which has flowed on. Therefore a river can visually replicate what's happened before, like our minds can, and its past is always out there, invisible, waiting to come back somewhere new …

These droplets I dip my fingers into could have been drunk by snow leopards, and bedecked mountains like jewels. And now here in Somerset, if I listen carefully – open my ears to the landscape – I can guess at the gurgles and imagine all the lives they have been through, and I think they would like to tell me this if they could.

I cup my hands and fill them with liquid stories – drink them down and see if my veins now sing with adventure and whispers or the soft quietness of distant hills and the endless depth of rocks.

Hands wiped on old cords, I tighten my laces and walk on.

There was a time when I felt the call of cities. There was a time when I did not. But always through this there were the valleys and the hills. The glacier of roots creaking its way down the slopes to find me and catch my toes and remind me that this is the place where brains work best. Where the things to do find you in the absence of prescribed activity.

Stay still. Watch a little. Listen with real ears and train your eyes to the level of molehills. Things will look different.

Summer-twisting roads to high-up heathered hills, the moors stretch their way to the sea, dappled with neon-horned sheep as if strayed from a feral nightclub, a woollen rave of rain and sun in alternate flashes of light.

(In the city I hunted out hidden green spaces – a grave-yard for abandoned pedalos and ice cream vans was awash with foxes and squirrels.)

There are no people if you don't want there to be. Walkers take the known paths and it is only a little way to the passages of non-human creatures. Just outside the village the paths are too steep and pheasant fattened. There are no maps. Walking is an art of guesswork and embracing getting lost.

Down below the river is flecked with tiger light and the paint splashes of dragonfly dives. Their glints reflect up into the air and become day-stars. A hundred little suns.

There are birds in my head making nests of leaves and dream feathers.

Mud cradles my boots but I do not fall – it is good to go slowly, to drink it all in. I am tipsy on moors and woods and steep valleys. The bandits are gone into history, with aurochs and drowned forests. The salt marshes sing of them to crows, their memory bloats samphire – that's why it tastes so good I think. Taste buds remembering. Smells trigger hints of past lives – down by the sea the air is laced with salt and a distant touch of vinegar and greased paper. Those who ate the chips are long gone but the sky remembers their scent.

There was once a lady who fell in love with the moors and the forests and decided to never leave. She roamed all day till she knew the area better than the men with the maps; her feet felt the earth and her senses thrown out drew in the whole landscape as if sucking its beauty with a straw. Her mind held it like old photos. I sometimes wonder if I could become like her. Forget everything else and just be here – become part of this West Country wilderness. Fluttering.

Every spring I must be here to roll in the flowers. The sapphire sea of petals revealing itself from under new leaves that glow like an eiderdown of illuminated green bottles. Zigzagging the bank, this different city, this favela of flowers clings, hugs, creates petal buildings from scratch with mortar of dew and foundations of earthworms.

The suburbs of ferns lick words into the sky; with frilled tongues they write the air – essay the path in front of me.

Places want you to read their history you know. Memories are always everywhere in earth. They are highlighted by blue-light lamp posts, flower sentinels to watch what happens here, a temporary illumination like an old religious manuscript – a book of bells traipsing the rain-washed streets.

This library of trees aches lignified flames to the sky – upside-down tangles of pages, a natural shredder for myths.

I remember you.

I lie down on the damp dark ground and let the sun dapple me, and words drip from twigs on to my thirsty tongue.

Somerset falls in heart ribbons.

My tummy was torn open once, like a rock full of crystals. But now, softly here, the woods stitch it up again, stuff it with leaf wadding, kiss it better with bluebells.

The Wilderness
ANNA MCNUFF

I set out to conquer the wilderness today,
I was steadfast in my stride,
Mind's fire so determined,
Ambition at my side.

I grappled to her mountaintops,
Muddied the waters of her lakes,
Forced a path through her forests,
A trail of triumph in my wake.

Greedily, I gathered up her vistas,
And kept them as my own.
Cold and shiny trophies claimed,
Of places once unknown.

I stumbled through the wilderness today,
Her wind clawed at my face,
Icy rain made fingers numb,
As she watched me fall from grace.

She pinned me with thunderous cloud,
And gently held me there,
Empty tears over reddened cheeks,
Everything in me lain bare.

When morning came, the tears had dried,
She filled the sky with scarlet hues,
So that I might know her wonder,
So that I might pay my dues.

I took a walk with the wilderness today
And listened for the first time,
To the breath and rush of her oceans,
To her birdsong so divine.

All things once so familiar,
I now saw through fresh eyes,
Withered branches, buds still sleeping,
Beauty, in deep disguise.

I marvelled at the turquoise rivers,
Surging onwards in crusade,
Between granite banks, glowing amber,
As the days began to fade.

I lay down with the wilderness today,
Her warm earth spread across my back,
Each rough root and prickled branch,
All at once pressed flat.

Through a patchwork of blue and green,
A rustling canopy of leaves,
I stole glimpses of majestic eagles,
Who soared above the trees.

And when blue gave way to blackness,
Cut by a moon of silver light,
I watched a thousand starlets sparkle,
Through the quiet, sombre night.

I was still in the arms of the wilderness today,
And I let her soothe my soul.
For I had begun my journey broken,
And she had made me whole.

On the last day, each
step is precious. Mountains,
friends all fall away.

Trees turn into streets,
stone houses to concrete blocks,
as our boots trudge on.

A book full of stamps
held across a desk and no
more yellow arrows.

They're all here: snobs
spell-makers, loners, preachers
snorers, huggers, kin.

Snapshots from the Camino de Santiago
CATH DRAKE

About the Contributors

Jean Atkin

Jean Atkin walks most often in the Welsh Marches (but further afield whenever she can). She has published *Not Lost Since Last Time* (Oversteps Books), five poetry pamphlets and a children's novel. Her recent work appears in *The Interpreter's House*, *Magma*, *Lighthouse*, *Agenda*, *Ambit* and *Poetry Salzburg*. She is poet in residence for Hargate Primary School in West Bromwich and works regularly in schools and on community projects in partnership with a wide variety of organisations.

Polly Atkin

Polly Atkin lives in Cumbria. Her first poetry collection, *Basic Nest Architecture*, was published by Seren in 2017, following pamphlets *Bone Song* (Aussteiger, 2008) – shortlisted for the Michael Marks poetry pamphlet award in 2009, and *Shadow Dispatches* (Seren, 2013) – winner of the Mslexia pamphlet prize in 2012. She has taught English and creative writing at the universities of Strathclyde, Cumbria and Lancaster. She is a Penguin Random House WriteNow mentee for a forthcoming non-fiction book reflecting on place, belonging and chronic illness.

Camilla Barnard

Camilla Barnard is an editor for Vertebrate Publishing and loves to climb, walk and generally be immersed in the outdoors. She is a keen dotwork illustrator in her spare time and also enjoys practising yoga, reading and experimenting with various art mediums. She has worked on many of Vertebrate's most successful titles, including *There is No Map in Hell* by Steve Birkinshaw and *The Magician's Glass* by Ed Douglas.

Hazel Barnard

Hazel Barnard lives in Sussex and is primarily a botanical illustrator, her preferred medium being watercolours. Her other favourite subject matter includes landscapes – both present and past – historical architecture, insects and animals. Hazel regularly exhibits and sells her work, and she recently featured in an exhibition focusing on the work and influences of Capability Brown. Now retired, Hazel hopes to experiment with new mediums including lino print techniques. She is an active member of her local art, history and archaeology societies.

Sandy Bennett-Haber

Sandy Bennett-Haber is an Edinburgh-based Australian writer, mother and traveller who prefers barefoot exploring where the climate allows. She is the editor of *You Won't Remember This: Travel with Babies*, and a founder member of the Women Writers Network. Sandy has had short stories published in the UK and Australia, and has written for Travelettes, *Lothian Life*, Dear Damsels and Edinburgh Gossip Girls.

Jen Benson

Jen Benson is a full-time writer, full-time athlete and full-time mum. She usually co-authors with husband, Sim, and their books include two of the Day Walks series from Vertebrate (Devon and Cornwall); *The Adventurer's Guide to Britain* (2018); *Amazing Family Adventures* (2017); and *Wild Running* (2014). Jen and Sim write about nature, families, sport and adventures and also take all their own photos, usually with their two young children just out of shot. In 2015 they spent a year living under canvas, exploring Britain's national parks and wild places.

Judith Brown

Judith Brown has lived in the Lake District for thirty years, nurturing her passions: mountaineering, the natural world, history, t'ai chi and writing. Landscape and history are her key creative inspirations. She believes they form an important part of who we are. She finds how people interact with them physically, emotionally and spiritually endlessly fascinating. A founder member of Women Mountains Words, she has a handful of published articles and stories, including a collection shortlisted for the 2007 Boardman Tasker Award for Mountain Literature.

Claire Carter

Claire Carter is a writer, filmmaker and creative consultant, based between Sheffield and North Wales where she climbs, runs, and swims. She is the Artistic Director of Kendal Mountain Festival and the Engagement Officer for the Outdoor Industry Association. She has juried for Telluride Mountain Festival, Krakow Mountain Festival and SheExtreme Festival among others, and continues to work on the BMC's Women in Adventure Competition. Her first film, *Operation Moffat*, codirected with Jen Randall, followed the life of the first female British mountain guide and won twenty-one international festival awards. Claire sits on the Nature Connection Index Academic Group, and is investigating how the arts can contribute to our connection to nature, and allied empathy through her creative and corporate work.

Genevieve Carver

Genevieve Carver is a poet and surfer searching for the humanity amidst the chaos and seeking solace in the sea. Her work has previously been published in magazines and anthologies including *Iota*, *Envoi*, *The North* and *Wordlife 10*. Since 2016 she has been touring her show *The Unsung* with a live band: a tribute in poetry and sound to forgotten heroes who lost their lives to music, which she also released as a studio album and book in 2017.

Imogen Cassels

Imogen Cassels is from Sheffield and studies in Cambridge. Her poems have been featured or are forthcoming in the *London Review of Books*, *Blackbox Manifold*, *Ambit*, *Datableed*, *No Prizes*, *The London Magazine* and on the London Underground.

Maria Coffey

Maria Coffey is an internationally published author of twelve books. Her first book, *Fragile Edge*, won two prizes in Italy. *Where the Mountain Casts its Shadow* won the Jon Whyte Award for mountain literature at the 2003 Banff Mountain Book Festival and a 2004 National Outdoor Book Award. For her contribution to mountain literature, including her most recent book *Explorers of the Infinite*, Maria received the 2009 American Alpine Club's H. Adams Carter Literary Award. Maria and her husband Dag Goering co-founded Hidden Places, a boutique adventure travel company that also fundraises for the conservation of elephants and other endangered species. Their home base is on Vancouver Island, BC.

Lee Craigie

Lee Craigie was an outdoor instructor and child counsellor before turning full-time mountain bike racer. She was the British mountain bike champion in 2013, a member of Team GB at the world and European championships and represented Scotland at the 2014 Commonwealth Games, but the secret to her sporting success lies in her love of exploring big mountains by bike. Fascinated by the places we can take ourselves emotionally by pushing our perceived limits, Lee now rides long distances through wild places self-supported by bike. She is also passionate about fair representation in sport and established The Adventure Syndicate in an effort to offer an alternative female sporting role model. She lives in Inverness, in her van or on her bike.

Joanna Croston

Joanna grew up and went to university in Eastern Canada and moved to the Canadian Rockies permanently in 1998. She has climbed many of the classic 11,000-foot peaks in the area and is an avid backcountry skier having skied throughout North America, the Alps, Kashmir and the Indian Himalaya. As a voracious reader of mountain literature and film enthusiast, she is the Programming Director for the Banff Mountain Film and Book Festival. Her writing has appeared in *Highline* magazine, *Gripped*, the *Canadian Alpine Journal* and *Alpinist*. She also serves on the Mountain Culture Committee of the Alpine Club of Canada and is a representative for the International Alliance for Mountain Film.

Lizzy Dalton

Lizzy Dalton is an artist based in Portland, Oregon. Originally from New York, she recently moved to the western USA to be closer to the places that inspire her most. Lizzy enjoys experimenting with different media, but mostly works in pen and paint on paper, creating meticulously detailed pieces that combine decorative and naturalistic forms.

She is largely inspired by her experiences as a climber and hiker, focusing on the sense of connection she feels to the outdoors. Lizzy studied studio art at Wesleyan University in Connecticut.

Nick Davies

Nick Davies has spent many years as an art director and completed a Masters in fine art in 2015, which initiated a curiosity with transitory movements in natural phenomena. Inspired by her coastal location and rural landscape in South Wales, Nick's arts practice is informed by nature, and it is her aim to look at re-integrating nature into art through capturing the energy and rhythm of the natural world. Nick has been involved in art facilitation within educational establishments and as an independent visual artist. She has exhibited her art since 2008 and has been invited to be a part of solo and collaborative exhibitions.

Heather Dawe

Heather Dawe is a writer, painter, cyclist and runner and lives in Yorkshire with her partner and young family. A previous winner of the Three Peaks Cyclo-Cross, Helvellyn Triathlon and a number of mountain marathons, she works as a data scientist and has founded a leading healthcare analytics consultancy. Her first book, *Adventures in Mind*, was published in 2013 and her second, *A Bicycle Ride in Yorkshire*, in 2014. Her paintings and prints have been exhibited around the North of England. She finds inspiration in the time she spends running and cycling in the mountains and other wild places. As her daughters grow, she increasingly shares adventures in the hills with them.

Cath Drake

Cath Drake is an Australian from Perth who lives in London. Cath has been published in anthologies and literary magazines in the UK, Australia and the US. Cath's pamphlet *Sleeping with Rivers* won the 2013 Mslexia/Seren poetry pamphlet prize and was the Poetry Book Society summer choice in 2014. She was included in *The Best Australian Poems 2014* anthology shortlisted for the 2015 Manchester Poetry Prize and came second in the 2017 Resurgence Poetry Prize. She will be writer in residence at the Katharine Susannah Prichard Writers' Centre in Australia in 2018. She is also a copywriter and non-fiction writer and her work includes award-winning journalism and PR, writing for radio, oral history and life stories. Cath is also a mindfulness teacher.

Paula Dunn

Paula Dunn is a Yorkshire-based artist whose atmospheric paintings are inspired by the dramatic northern landscapes of Britain. She currently works from her home studio, which is based in the beautiful, inspiring World Heritage village of Saltaire, West Yorkshire. She is a landscape painter who works with oils and paints in response to places she has walked and explored: Scotland, Ireland, Iceland, the Lake District and Yorkshire, where she currently lives. Her work is very much influenced by light, colours and textures; she experiments with techniques such as impasto, mark making and developing layers with glazes and cold wax infused with dry pigments. Paula paints landscapes inspired by feelings and memories of a place and at a particular point in time. Her paintings respond to the weather and other natural forces that have an influence on the landscape.

Lily Dyu

Lily Dyu was born in Ireland, grew up in England, lives in Wales and spends most of her holidays in Scotland. A keen runner and cyclist she has fastpacked and bike-toured extensively: from the sheep trods and muddy lanes of home, to the sky-high trails and loftiest roads of the Himalaya. She still loves the buzz of a big city marathon, but she's always happiest when she's outdoors with friends and preferably in lumpy places.

Caroline Eustace

Caroline has always enjoyed recording on paper the enormity of the landscape and weather, with the close-up details at her feet, whether the experience is from around the world or in her back garden, and has exhibited her work at the Brewery Arts Centre in Kendal. She has worked in national parks, art galleries, museums and schools, including the Lake District National Park Authority visitor centre at Brockhole, Windermere; Lakeland Arts at Abbot Hall Art Gallery;

Blackwell, The Arts & Crafts House, and Natural England among others, enabling people to explore and develop practices reflective of their immediate experiences of the world.

Hazel Findlay

Hazel Findlay has been rock climbing for twenty-two of her twenty-eight years. She has travelled all over the world climbing all styles from small boulders to big walls. As a child she competed, but gave that up at sixteen to spend more time outdoors having adventures. After graduating from the University of Bristol with a 2:1 in philosophy she started a career as a professional climber. Hazel is better known for more adventurous trad climbing. She was the first British woman to climb E9, the first British woman to free-climb El Capitan in Yosemite and has put up first ascents all over the world. She is also one of the top female sport climbers in the UK; with her ascent of *Fish Eye* she was the first British woman to climb 8c. With a strong passion for teaching and psychology she has started breaking ground in coaching mental training for climbers. In all her adventures and passions Hazel is most driven by personal development, learning and growth.

Paula Flach

Paula Flach is an editor, illustrator, runner, lover of salt liquorice and riddles. Born to a potter and an art teacher in southern Germany, she grew up surrounded by colours, clay, paper and her two brothers. During her studies of visual culture and film in Norway, she discovered the best adventure park she knows: the Norwegian wilderness. Back in Munich, Paula works as an editorial programmer for the European Outdoor Film Tour and the International Ocean Film Tour. Her work has been shown in several exhibitions.

Anna Fleming

Anna Fleming is a writer from Mid Wales. She works for the Cairngorms National Park and writes a blog about mountains, culture and environment called The Granite Sea. She is leading a mountaineering oral history project, collecting stories from some of the pioneering mountaineers in the Cairngorms. Her doctoral research examined Wordsworth and Cumbrian communities.

Nikki Frumkin

Nikki Frumkin is an artist and alpinist based in Seattle, Washington. Her work is inspired by time spent hiking, climbing and mountaineering in the beautiful Pacific Northwest. She is drawn to rugged, remote and wild places. Her paper and watercolours come with her on her human-powered adventures, small paper tucked into her pocket on big adventures or enormous sheets strapped to the outside of her pack like a sail. Her paintings have been exhibited in shows across the country. She also creates art and design work within the climbing and outdoor industry.

Claire Giordano

Claire Giordano is a painter, illustrator, alpinist and writer based in the forested foothills outside Seattle, Washington. She completed her undergraduate degrees at Seattle University in environmental education and communication, and philosophy. Claire's commercial work includes a bestselling T-shirt design for REI's Force of Nature campaign, hand-painted maps, and custom ski top-sheet designs. She also collaborates with local scientists to blend art and data. You are most likely to find Claire on a ski slope or perched beside a trail, paintbrush in one hand and a chocolate bar in the other.

Alison Grant

Alison Grant is a landscape architect who lives in Inverness, from where she has great access to the hills of the north and west. Her writing has been published in a number of anthologies and magazines, including *New Writing Scotland*, *Gutter Magazine* and *A Wilder Vein*, an anthology of writing about wild places.

Geraldine Green

Geraldine Green is a UK writer, tutor and poetry editor and has two full poetry collections: *The Other Side of the Bridge*, and *Salt Road*, published by Indigo Dreams Publishing. Her work has been widely anthologised in the UK and the USA. A frequent visitor to North America, in 2015 she celebrated ten years of poetry readings there. In 2011 she gained a PhD in creative writing from the University of Lancaster titled 'An Exploration of Identity and Environment through Poetry'. Her third full collection, *Passing Through*, was published in 2018 by Indigo Dreams. Geraldine writes a blog entitled Geraldine Green Salt Road.

Lilace Mellin Guignard

Lilace Mellin Guignard lives with her husband and two children in rural Pennsylvania, where she teaches creative writing, women's studies, and outdoor recreation leadership at Mansfield University. Her poetry has appeared in many journals and anthologies, including *Poetry* magazine. She has published a poetry chapbook, *Young at the Time of Letting Go*, and her book about women outdoors is forthcoming from Texas A&M Press. Lilace writes a blog entitled A Tent of One's Own.

Alyson Hallett

Alyson Hallett's latest book is *Lzrd*, co-written with Penelope Shuttle. Her other books include *Walking Stumbling Limping Falling* (2017), *Geographical Intimacy* (2016), *Suddenly Everything* (2013), *The Stone Library* (2009) and *The Heart's Elliptical Orbit* (2003). Her pamphlet, *Toots*, was shortlisted for the 2017 Michael Marks award. Alyson has made drama and an audio diary for BBC Radio 4 and an essay for BBC Radio 3. She lives near Bath and has been curating the international poetry as public art project, The Migration Habits of Stones, for the past seventeen years.

Melissa Harrison

Melissa Harrison is an author and critic. Her books have been shortlisted for prizes including the Costa novel of the year award, and longlisted for prizes including the Baileys Women's Prize for Fiction, the Encore Award and the Wainwright Prize. Melissa writes a monthly Nature Notebook column in *The Times* and reviews books for publications including the *Financial Times*, *The Times*, *The Guardian*, and *Slightly Foxed*.

Kathryn Hummel

Kathryn Hummel is the author of *Poems from Here*, *The Bangalore Set*, *The Body That Holds*, *splashback* and *Lamentville*. Uncollected, her digital media/poetry, non-fiction, fiction and scholarly research has been published and presented worldwide, and recognised with a Pushcart Prize nomination (2013) and the Dorothy Porter Award for Poetry (2013). Kathryn holds a PhD for studies in narrative ethnography, lives intermittently in South Asia and edits 'Travel/Write/Translation' for Australian journal *Verity La*.

Katie Ives

Katie Ives is the editor-in-chief of *Alpinist*. She is a graduate of the University of Iowa Writers' Workshop and the Banff Mountain and Wilderness Writing Program. Her work has appeared in a variety of publications, including *The New York Times*, *Outside* and *Rock, Paper, Fire: The Best of Mountain and Wilderness Writing*. In 2016 she received the American Alpine Club's H. Adams Carter Literary Award, and one of her *Alpinist* articles made the Notables list for Best American Sports Writing.

Kathleen Jones

Kathleen Jones is a poet, biographer and novelist, whose subjects include Katherine Mansfield, Norman Nicholson and Christina Rossetti. Her account of the lives of the women associated with the Lake Poets, *A Passionate Sisterhood*, was a Virago Classic. Kathleen worked in broadcast journalism and is the author of two novels, a collection of short fiction and four collections of poetry. She has taught creative writing in a number of universities, is a Royal Literary Fund fellow, and in 2012 was elected a fellow of the English Association.

Mab Jones

Mab Jones is a 'unique talent' (*The Times*) who has read her work all over the UK, in the USA, France, Ireland and Japan. She is winner of the John Tripp Spoken Poetry audience award, the Word Factory Neil Gaiman short story competition, the Aurora Poetry Prize, the Rabbit Heart Poetry Film Festival Grand Jury Prize, and the Geoff Stevens Memorial Poetry Prize, among others. Her most recent collection, *take your experience and peel it*, is published by Indigo Dreams. Her first collection, *Poor Queen*, was published by Burning Eye Books. She teaches creative writing at Cardiff University, writes for the *New York Times*, and has presented three poetry programmes on BBC Radio 4, the most recent in 2018. She also coordinates International Dylan Thomas Day.

Solana Joy

Solana Joy grew up in Alaska and has spent most of her adult years migrating back and forth across the Atlantic. Her writing has appeared in a range of British, Irish and American publications. In addition to essays, she is currently working on a novel and a memoir about travelling the world with her feline sidekick. Her nomadic life of writing and cat-schlepping is held together with knitting, music, comedy, books, Zen, tea and sturdy zippers.

Dr Judy Kendall

Judy Kendall is Reader in English and creative writing at the University of Salford, an award-winning poet and visual text exponent. Her poetry books are *insatiable carrot* (visual gardening), *Climbing Postcards* (climbing poetry), *Joy Change* (inspired by seven years in Japan), and *The Drier The Brighter* – all published by Cinnamon Press. Two extended 2017 visual poems feature wandering through Pennine landscapes and transient territories of translation: *Mismapping* (*What Lies Within*, Liquorice Fish Books), and *brief brief* (*Versal*, Amsterdam's literary and arts journal).

Tami Knight

Tami Knight has been drawing cartoons about climbers since the early 1980s. Canadian west coaster Tami asks, through a mouthful of chocolate, '*Why izzint there more humour in climbing lit? … it's like shooting fish in a barrel.*' In real life, Knight teaches children how not to fall on their heads and always remembers to feed her cat.

She had a regular cartoon feature in *Climbing* magazine from 1994 to 2004, and semi-regularly in *Alpinist* magazine since its inception, including a feature on Squamish climbing in issue 43. Tami was the American Alpine Club Literary Award winner in 2003, has written seven books and illustrated twenty more. *Everest: The Ultimate Hump* was shortlisted at the Banff Mountain Book Festival in 2000.

Anja Konig

Anja Konig grew up in the German language and now writes in English. Her first pamphlet *Advice for an Only Child* was shortlisted for the 2015 Michael Marks award. *Some Cannot be Caught*, an anthology of animal poetry co-edited with Liane Strauss, was published by Emma Press in May 2018. Most weekends Anja is up in the Alps with Horst, their tent and two bags of dried pasta.

Tara Kramer

Tara Kramer's love of wide expanses and broad horizons began during childhood in the cornfields of eastern Iowa. She's spent the last decade working for the USA Polar Programs and Polar Bears International at field sites throughout Greenland, Antarctica and Canada. She devotes most other moments to exploring quiet wild spaces. Continuously torn between faraway adventures and a strong cup of coffee in her own kitchen, she's currently based in Bozeman, Montana with her long-time love, Nick.

Dr Alexandra Lewis

Dr Alexandra Lewis is Lecturer in English Literature, and Associate Director of the Centre for the Novel, at the University of Aberdeen. She is editor of *Wuthering Heights: Norton Critical Edition* and *The Brontës and the Idea of the Human* (Cambridge University Press, 2018), and has published extensively on literature and psychology. Alexandra received her PhD from the University of Cambridge, Trinity College, where she was a Cambridge Commonwealth Trust Scholar, and her BA (Hons) from the University of Sydney, where she was University Medallist in English. Before taking up her lectureship at Aberdeen she taught English Literature at several Cambridge colleges; Goldsmiths, University of London; and the University of Warwick. She serves on the executive committee of both the British and the Australasian Associations for Victorian Studies. Alexandra's poetry and fiction appear in *Causeway/Cabhsair*, *The Interpreter's House* and *Southerly*.

Tessa Lyons

Tessa Lyons is a landscape artist and illustrator best known for her work within the outdoor industry. Most notably her work was shortlisted for the prestigious Haworth Prize at the Mall Galleries in London in 2016. In 2017 she was invited to carry out a residency at the Banff Centre for Arts and Creativity in Canada. Her work has appeared in a variety of publications and media as she continues to work closely with organisations that share her passion for the outdoors at the heart of their initiatives, including: the British Mountaineering Council, National Trust, Banff Mountain Film and Book Festival, Kendal Mountain Festival, Lowe Alpine, Mountain Equipment, *Alpinist* magazine and *Rock and Ice* magazine.

Alice Maddicott

Alice Maddicott is a writer, artist and creative education practitioner from Somerset. Over the past decade her published work has spanned everything from poetry to children's television scripts for CBeebies; from public art commissions to travel writing. She has performed at home and abroad, including at the 2013 Belgrade Poetry Festival. In 2009 she was writer in residence for the 60th anniversary of the Yorkshire Dales National Park. She currently runs the Young Writers' Lab for Bath Festivals and works extensively in schools, as well as on a number of creative projects across the West Country.

Bernadette McDonald

Bernadette McDonald is the author of ten mountaineering books, including the multi-award-winning *Art of Freedom* (2017). Among its international awards, *Art of Freedom* won the Mountain Literature Award at the Banff Mountain Book Festival, the Boardman Tasker Award for Mountain Literature and the National Outdoor Book Award for Biography. Her other mountaineering titles include *Tomaž Humar* (2008), *Brotherhood of the Rope: The Biography of Charles Houston* (2007), *Freedom Climbers* (2011), *Keeper of the Mountains: The Elizabeth Hawley Story* (2012), and *Alpine Warriors* (2015). She has also received the Alberta Order of Excellence (2010), the Summit of Excellence Award (2007) and the King Albert Award for international leadership in mountain culture and environment (2006). She was the founding vice-president of Mountain culture at the Banff Centre and served as director of the Banff mountain festivals from 1988–2006.

Anna McNuff

Anna McNuff is an endurance athlete, adventurer and mischief maker. Named by *The Guardian* as one of the top female adventurers of our time, *Condé Nast Traveler* has recently included her in a list of the fifty most influential travellers in the world. She is the UK ambassador for Girlguiding, and has cycled over 20,000 miles in Europe and the Americas, including through all fifty states of the USA. She has also run the length of New Zealand and has a penchant for rollerblading.

Helen Mort

Helen Mort is a writer, trail runner and climber who lives in Sheffield. She teaches creative writing at Manchester Metropolitan University and has published two poetry collections with Chatto & Windus. Her latest, *No Map Could Show Them*, explores the history of women's mountaineering. She has been shortlisted for the Costa prize and the T.S. Eliot prize, and in 2014 won the Fenton Aldeburgh First Collection prize. Her first novel is forthcoming from Chatto in 2019. She is also the author of *Lake District Trail Running* and has written for *Alpinist* and *Climb*. In 2017, she was a judge for the Man Booker International Prize, and chair of judges for the Boardman Tasker Award for Mountain Literature.

Kari Nielsen

Kari Nielsen earned a BA in English from Middlebury College and has attended the Bread Loaf Writers' Conference. In recent years, she has guided wilderness trips and managed remote properties in Utah, Alaska and Chilean Patagonia. Kari currently works as a wilderness ranger in Montana, where she lives with her husband, Christian.

Leslie Hsu Oh

Leslie Hsu Oh is a White House Champion of Change for AAPI Storytelling and Art, a Schweitzer fellow, and the Outdoor Editor for *Panorama: The Journal of Intelligent Travel*. Known for her love of mountains and taking her young kids on extreme adventures, Leslie is a writer of fiction and non-fiction whose work has been named among the distinguished stories of the year by Best American Essays. Her award-winning writing and photography has appeared or is forthcoming in *Alpinist*, *Backpacker*, *Condé Nast Traveler*, *Fourth Genre*, *Outside*, *Parenting*, *Real Simple*, *Smithsonian*, *Sierra*, *Travel + Leisure*, and the *Washington Post*. Leslie has a Master's degree from Harvard, an MFA from the University of Alaska, and has taught creative writing for over a decade. She is currently working on a memoir entitled *Fireweed*, which features the four sacred mountains surrounding Navajo lands.

Evelyn O'Malley

Evelyn O'Malley is a lecturer in drama at the University of Exeter. She is interested in weather and weathering, responses to climatic and environmental change, inequality and migration, and theatre and performance. She is currently working on a book, *Weathering Shakespeare*, for Bloomsbury's Environmental Cultures series, alongside two sea-related projects. *Taking the Ferry* concerns abortion travel from Ireland, and *Dancing as the Tide Comes In* responds to global sea-level rise. Favourite adventures include beach trips with Tio the spaniel and cycling round the city on a rusty bike.

Sarah Outen

Sarah Outen is an adventurer by land and sea, and has spent most of the last decade either on or telling stories about her remote expeditions. Sarah is generally happiest when wandering, roaming or just being in the wild. Her ideal night out would be round the campfire with friends and a cheeky fruity gin. She's authored two books, the latest of which is *Dare to Do*. This recounts the tales of her four-and-a-half-year bid to row, cycle and kayak around the northern hemisphere. Her mission is to encourage others outside, especially youngsters.

Libby Peter

Libby Peter is at times a climber who runs, at others a runner who climbs. Ideally in the mountains, though the coast has an almost equal pull, the legacy of a Cornish childhood. By profession she is a mountain guide, which gives her yet another excuse to escape to wild places. But not always. She is also (and always) a mother. Climbing adventures with her daughters are high on her favourite-things list, though being out-climbed by them, less so!

Jen Randall

Jen Randall is a filmmaker with one foot in Scotland and the other in British Columbia. She is best known for documentaries about adventurous women, often exploring the links between identity and landscape. Jen frequently quests into the wilds on adventures inspired by her subjects, from long-distance walks to big-wall climbs.

Penelope Shuttle

Penelope Shuttle lives in Cornwall. Her collection *Will You Walk A Little Faster?* (Bloodaxe Books, 2017) was Poetry Book of the Month (July) in *The Observer*, and her latest publication is *Lzrd* (Indigo Dreams, 2018), poems about the Lizard Peninsula in Cornwall, in collaboration with Alyson Hallett.

Ruth Wiggins

Ruth Wiggins lives in London. Her work has appeared most recently in *Poetry Review* and *Poetry* (Chicago). Her pamphlet *Myrtle* was published by the Emma

Press in 2014 and she is currently working on a first collection concerning ideas around female self-reliance. A keen hiker, Ruth keeps a blog about poetry, travel and mud entitled Mudpath.

Allison Williams

Allison Williams holds degrees from Duke University and University of Alaska Anchorage, with studies at the University of Oxford and an ethnobiology field school. After eight years as a writer and editor in New York City, she became senior editor at *Seattle Met* in 2011. She is a climber, backcountry skier and author of three travel books. Her fiction thesis won the Jason Wenger Award for Literary Excellence and her work has been recognised by the Society of Professional Journalists and the City and Regional Magazine Association.

Pam Williamson

Pam Williamson is an artist living and working in the Lake District, and as such faces daily the challenge of creating fresh responses to a much-loved and recorded environment. So she walks, responding in drawings, words and later in paint, to the experiences of a day, a moment or an atmosphere. Her work evolves as series; recently in paint, *The Pass Book* and *36 Ways to see Scafell Pike*. She also creates mixed media installations. *Primal Scream*, *Watermark* and *StingJet* are recent responses to environmental extreme events in the Lake District.

Deziree Wilson

Deziree Wilson has spent much of her life exploring wild

environments on rock, snow or water and her artwork is inspired by her love of exploring wild and beautiful places. She tries to recreate the sensation and quality of these experiences: how rock feels under her fingers when she climbs it, the noise snow or ice makes when she skis across it, or the sensation of water as she swims through it. The figures within her drawings are immersed in and absorbed by their surroundings, and Deziree tries to represent that elemental relationship.

Krystle Wright

Krystle Wright is an adventure-sports photographer from Queensland, Australia, although she now lives a semi-nomadic lifestyle in her quest to capture and present unique moments from extreme sports, expeditions and adventures across the globe. Whether she's camping on a frozen fjord for a month in the Arctic with twenty-three BASE jumpers, paragliding in the Karakoram range in Pakistan or sleeping on the back of a yacht on the Great Barrier Reef, Krystle strives to pursue fresh challenges, to seek out undiscovered layers and dimensions in her work, and is recognised for her creativity, composition, and an indomitable spirit in the face of adversity. Krystle will do whatever it takes to shoot from her unique perspective – whether hanging from precarious positions on remote cliff edges, swimming through jagged, unexplored canyons, or trudging for days through vicious, baleful weather.

Acknowledgements

So many people came together to make this project what it is that it makes it very hard to write a definitive list, but we have endeavoured to do so, and hope that anyone whose name does not appear but feels it should knows that in our hearts we are thankful, but our memories have failed us on this occasion!

First and foremost, each and every artist, poet and writer must be thanked for donating their eloquent, inspired, often perceptive, in places humorous and always beautiful, contributions. Without the generosity of these talented, wild-hearted women we could not have made this small but vital step towards addressing the imbalance of female and male voices in the outdoor-adventure literary archives.

Thanks go to Melissa Harrison who took time out of a no-doubt extremely busy schedule to write a beautiful, sensitive and thoughtful introduction for *Waymaking*.

Tessa Lyons, Sheffield-based, exceptionally talented landscape artist, gifted the delicate and soulful part-title illustrations. Thank you, Tessa.

And last but absolutely not least, we would like to thank our partner Alpkit for their generous support of the *Waymaking* project.

The editors and publisher would like to thank the following people for their support of the *Waymaking* project:

Alasdair Alexander

Clare Archibald

Heather Theresa Bain

Stuart Banner

David Barlow

Hazel P. Barnard

Anne Bartle

Chris Bartle

Ella and Hannah Barty

Sejuti Basu

John Beatty

Jamie Lynn Bergstrom

bnwthrs

Marcela Bonilla

Sarah Boon

Andy Boorman

Ingrid Bridgman

Susan Buckingham

Alex Burton-Keeble

Christina Button

Susie Campbell

Linda Jane Canton

Wendy Carr

Fiona Chaloner

Abby Chilton

Steve Chilton

Becky Clark

Jennifer Clark

Nic Clarke

Hannah Collingridge

Bob Comlay

Jennie Condell

Amy Cooke

Lizzie Cooke

Helen Cooper

Neil Cottam

Charles Coull

Karen Darby

Frances Dawe

Noel Dawson

Nicola Dempsey

Paul Diffley

Wiblet A. Doblet

Ed Douglas

Loris Martin Doyle

Mandy Drake

Kate Durkacz

Lily Dyu

Christine Edmonds

Kate M. Eidam

Ben Emmens –
    The Conscious Project

Marion Esfandiari

Cath Evans

Julie Farina

Rose and Klaus Feikes

Michael Fenton

Footless Crow Mountain Life

Enid Forsyth

Kerena Fussell

Katharine Ganly

Glacier Books

Andy Gladdis

Greg Glade

Rita E. Gould

Megan Green

Rob Greenwood

Gemma Grewar

Anisha Grover

Holle Hahn

Rachel Hale

Ray Handford

Jane Harle

Karmen Harley

Nicky Harverson

Cecilia Haynes

Amy Heard

Matt Heason

Colin Hilton

Beki Hooper

Michelle Hordern

Suzy Horne

Georgina Jackson (2Travlrs)

Hazel Jones

Lizzie Kaye
Hetty Key
Susan Lafferty
Faye Latham
Alison Liedkie
Patrick Limb
Andrew Long
Darren James Longhorn
Chris Loynes
James MacIntosh
Elke Mack
Dr Rona Mackenzie
Geoffrey Mann
Andrew Marshall
Susanne Masters
Mark McBride
Debbie McCart
Claire McMullen
Paul McWhinney
Valerie Mitchell
Louisa Elisabeth Moore
Alison Morton
Jenni Virgo Muir
Meredith Muirhead
Hannah Mycock-Overell
Darrick Nielsen
John O'Reilly
Neasa O'Sullivan
Patrick O'Sullivan
ottero
Steven Pate
Abi and Isla Paulley
Nadia Permogorov
David Price

Paul Pritchard
Stephen Quinney
Pam Ranger Roberts
Ash Reber
Julia M. Renn
Jason Rhodes
Caroline Robinson
Cath Rodkoff
Hanke Roos
Lindsey Ross
Christian Rückl
Sue Savege
Bob A. Schelfhout Aubertijn
Marcus Scotney
Sue Scowcroft
Paul Scully
Marian Sharkey
Sarah Sharps
Shayna Skarf
Joseph Spuckler
Tom Stafford
David Steane
Benedict Steele
Katie Sutherland
Louise Sykes
Judith Symes
Emma Taylor
The Edinburgh Festival of Cycling
Emily Thompson
Tomo Thompson
Siffy Torkildson
Elizabeth Torres Ms Neverstop
Lesley Totten
Gemma Turner

Sir Twonkalot
Ruth Tym
Jinaka Ugochukwu
Keith Urry
Bregje van Veelen
Hannah J. Varacalli
Hanna Varga
Sally Vince
Tom W.
Graham Watson
Paul Watson
Tom Wellstead
Tony and Martha Whittome
Pete Wilkie
Morgan Williams
Yitka Winn
Howard Wix
Womenclimb
Kathryn Wood
Helen Woodhouse
Nadine Young
Angela